Côte d'Ivoire

Frontispiece: **Kola nuts**

Consultant: Abou B. Bamba, Associate Professor of History and Africana Studies, Gettysburg College, Gettysburg, Pennsylvania

Please note: All statistics are as up-to-date as possible at the time of publication.

Book production by The Design Lab

Library of Congress Cataloging-in-Publication Data
Names: Bjorklund, Ruth, author.
Title: Côte d'Ivoire (Ivory Coast) / by Ruth Bjorklund.
Description: New York : Children's Press, [2019] | Series: Enchantment of the
 world | Includes bibliographical references and index.
Identifiers: LCCN 2018019517 | ISBN 9780531126974 (library binding : alk.
 paper)
Subjects: LCSH: Côte d'Ivoire—Juvenile literature.
Classification: LCC DT545.22 .B57 2019 | DDC 966.68—dc23
LC record available at https://lccn.loc.gov/2018019517

Scholastic Inc., 557 Broadway, New York, NY 10012

1 2 3 4 5 6 7 8 9 10 R 28 27 26 25 24 23 22 21 20 19

Côte d'Ivoire

BY RUTH BJORKLUND

Enchantment of the World™
Second Series

CHILDREN'S PRESS®

An Imprint of Scholastic Inc.

Contents

CHAPTER I

Unity and Growth

Opposite: **People from Côte d'Ivoire often wear bright, patterned clothing.**

SCHOOL IS STARTING IN LESS THAN A WEEK. KOUASSI is looking forward to his second year of junior high. His sister, Amian, will be going into her first year at the *lycée*. Lycée means "high school" in French, the national language of Côte d'Ivoire, a nation in West Africa. Kouassi is especially excited today, because he and Amian are joining their mother on a short business trip. His mother owns a shop in Marcory, a suburb of Abidjan, Côte d'Ivoire's largest city. She sells arts and crafts, mainly to tourists. She does well, now that the war is over and the economy is growing. More tourists are visiting the beaches along the coast.

Kouassi's family lives in Marcory. The city is lush with palm trees and tropical flowers, but it is loud and crowded, too. The family moved to Abidjan when Kouassi was young. He was born in Bouaké. It is also a large city, but nothing like Abidjan.

An ivory warehouse in London, England. Trade in African elephant ivory was banned in 1990, but before then it was used to make products ranging from buttons to piano keys to sculpture.

What's in a Name?

Until the nineteenth century, Côte d'Ivoire did not exist as a single country. The region was made up of several kingdoms. In the fifteenth century, Portuguese merchants began trading along the coast of West Africa. They labeled each region according to the trade goods they found there. Elephants roamed most of what is now Côte d'Ivoire and the local people traded primarily in elephant tusk ivory. Thus, the Portuguese called that section of the West African coast Costa do Marfim, meaning Ivory Coast. In the nineteenth century, the French laid claim on the region and called it Côte d'Ivoire, French for Ivory Coast. For more than a century, the country was known around the world as the Ivory Coast. In 1985, the Ivoirian government requested that the country be officially called Côte d'Ivoire in all languages, so the United States now refers to the country as Côte d'Ivoire.

Abidjan is along the southern coast of Côte d'Ivoire. The city is built on several peninsulas surrounded by the Ébrié Lagoon, a long, narrow turquoise waterway that separates the coast from the Atlantic Ocean. Huge office towers, hotels, restaurants, shops, galleries, and museums make up the center of the city, called Le Plateau. Not many people live in Le Plateau, but many work there. Most residents live in suburbs surrounding the city such as Cocody, Yopougon, and Marcory. Traffic is terrible in Abidjan. The city is divided in half by the lagoon, and people can spend hours each day waiting to cross the Félix Houphouët-Boigny Bridge. The bridge, which connects the two halves of Abidjan, is named after the country's first president.

Beginning in the nineteenth century, Côte d'Ivoire was a French colony. It did not become independent until 1960. Houphouët-Boigny was president for more than thirty years, and during that time the country grew prosperous. But after he died, competing groups disrupted the country's peace. Citizens took sides, and in 2002, Côte d'Ivoire went to war with itself. Rebel armies in the north took over most of the northern cities and based themselves in the city of Bouaké. From Bouaké, they marched south to Abidjan. Many people were killed and others fled the country. Cease-fires came and went, until finally, in 2007, a peace treaty was signed.

By this time, Kouassi's parents were ready to leave Bouaké. All around them, homes were riddled with bullet holes. Historic colonial buildings were left in ruins. Schools and markets were destroyed and many neighborhoods were without electricity and clean water.

Before the war, Kouassi's parents had owned a small textile business. They bought cotton from local farmers and hired weavers to make cloth. They decided to move to Marcory because it seemed safe and much of it had been rebuilt after the war. Streets were repaved and power lines were restored. Everyone considered themselves fortunate. Kouassi's father found a job working for a cotton exporting company. Now that the war was over, Côte d'Ivoire's economy was slowly recovering, and Abidjan was growing.

But in 2010, disaster struck again. Côte d'Ivoire had held a presidential election. The winner, Alassane Ouattara, was elected, but the incumbent president, Laurent Gbagbo,

refused to leave office. Again, political enemies created armies. Again, the armies fought, destroyed buildings, and killed thousands. Mercifully, peace was restored in 2011, and Côte d'Ivoire began its recovery from war one more time.

Kouassi eventually started school. He knew he was luckier than most children. Côte d'Ivoire had never had enough teachers or schools, and after years of civil war, there were fewer still. Some children, especially village children, do not go to school. Instead, they work with their parents. Some children work for their parents in markets or on farms. The children who work the hardest are those who work on the

A man walks through a house destroyed during Côte d'Ivoire's second civil war. Thousands of people were killed in the violence.

cocoa plantations. Cocoa trees produce about forty cocoa bean pods a year. Inside each pod are about thirty long, purple beans covered in a sticky pulp. Children clean the beans and put them in large, heavy burlap sacks. It is these beans that are used as the basis of making chocolate.

Both Amian and Kouassi are grateful to live in the city. There are schools in their neighborhood. They have desks, a teacher, and their parents can afford school supplies and classroom fees. The wars are behind them. Ivoirians want unity and a better life for all. Abidjan is growing, and Kouassi's parents' shop is thriving.

Kouassi's mother's business trip is to Korhogo, the chief market town of the Senufo ethnic group. The first Senufo people came to Côte d'Ivoire more than a thousand years ago. Senufo artisans are talented painters, potters, and woodcarvers.

Their skills are passed down from parent to child. The Senufo people are known around the world for their specialty hand-woven, hand-painted cloth known as Korhogo cloth.

The marketplace is bursting with sound and color. West African clothing is bright and colorful. Women wear headscarves and long wraparound skirts called *pagnes*. Often, mothers and daughters wear matching dresses. Men wear colorful patterned shirts or robes, and many wear skullcaps. Most boys wear Western-style shirts and shorts.

The wealth of the region is available at the market—fruits, vegetables, meat, crafts, tools, and everyday household goods. Kouassi's mother has come to buy Korhogo cloth, pottery, and beads for her shop. Walking through the market, she stops at a stall where two women are selling their pottery. Only women make pottery in Senufo villages. They dig up the clay soil and mix it with small stones and chipped pieces of old pottery. They do not use potter's wheels, but rather build the pots with coils of clay. After making the pots, the women put them on a large bonfire to harden them.

After a long day of shopping, Kouassi and his family fly to Bouaké. Kouassi looks down from the plane and watches the landscape below him change, from grasslands to green fields, rivers, and the edge of the rain forest. Everyone is looking forward to being with family. Kouassi's family is Baoulé, an ethnic group belonging to the Akan people, the largest in the country. When they arrive in Bouaké, a roomful of extended family will be waiting for them, and a table will be set with a mouthwatering array of foods. It will be good to be home.

CHAPTER 2

A Lush Landscape

F ROM THE AIR, CÔTE D'IVOIRE IS A LUSH, GREEN MASS of land crisscrossed by blue rivers and streams. Lakes and lagoons dot the landscape, and a long strip of white sand beach runs the length of the coastline. Côte d'Ivoire contains savannas, hills, tropical forests, and wetlands. Once called the Jewel of West Africa, Côte d'Ivoire has areas that have been damaged by overuse of natural resources. Today, however, many Ivoirians are working to heal and protect their beautiful country.

Opposite: **A bridge made of liana vines crosses the Cavally River in western Côte d'Ivoire.**

A West African Nation

Côte d'Ivoire belongs to the region of Africa known as West Africa. It is a medium-sized country, slightly larger than the U.S. state of New Mexico. To the south, Côte d'Ivoire has a long coastline along the Gulf of Guinea, a part of the Atlantic

Côte d'Ivoire's Geographic Features

Area: 124,502 square miles (322,460 sq km)

Average High Temperature: In Yamoussoukro, 85°F (30°C) in February, 78°F (25.5°C) in August

Average Low Temperature: In Yamoussoukro, 77°F (25°C) in February, 73°F (23°C) in August

Average Annual Precipitation: Yamoussoukro, 44 inches (112 cm)

Highest Elevation: Mount Nimba, 5,748 feet (1,752 m) above sea level

Lowest Elevation: Sea level along the coast

Longest River: Bandama, about 500 miles (800 km)

Length of Coastline: 322 miles (518 km)

Average Annual Ocean Temperature: 82°F (28°C)

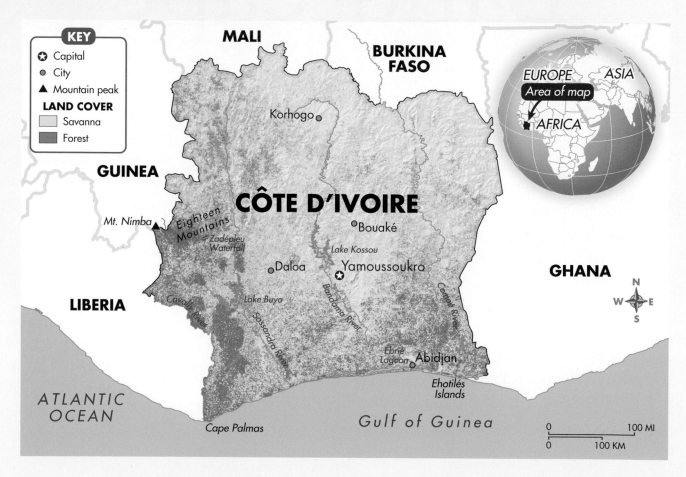

Ocean. To the west, Côte d'Ivoire shares a border with Liberia and Guinea, to the north, it borders Mali and Burkina Faso, and to the east, Ghana.

Houses in Abidjan line the shore.

From Plains to Mountains

Côte d'Ivoire can be divided into three geographic zones. Plains cover the southern half of the country. The area is flat and wet. The plains include the coast, which is made up of white sand-covered beaches and a few reefs and rock outcroppings. There are no natural harbors. A steep underwater shelf is located offshore, but the ocean is shallow once it reaches the beach. Incoming waves are large and powerful, and in most areas, too hazardous for swimming.

One of the highest points in Côte d'Ivoire is the Dent de Man, which means the "Tooth of Man." The rocky outcrop rises above a forested ridge of mountains in western Côte d'Ivoire, near the city of Man.

The coastal area also includes mangrove forests, marshes, swamps, and lagoons. The Ehotilés Islands marine park separates the Ébrié Lagoon from the heavy surf of the Atlantic Ocean. The lagoon's calmer waters protect the city of Abidjan and other towns such as Grand-Bassam and Bingerville. Beyond the coastal wetlands are stands of tropical evergreen forest. This area, once home to one of Africa's greatest tropical rain forests, has been largely replaced by farms and plantations.

North and central Côte d'Ivoire consist of low hills covered in a grassy landscape. In this region, tall grasses, bushes, and herbs grow beneath deciduous trees and palms.

Rising seas are destroying the land in Grand-Lahou, causing trees and buildings to collapse.

The Changing Coastline

Fishers, farmers, harbor workers, and tourists all rely on the health of the Gulf of Guinea, but global climate change is endangering the gulf.

In Côte d'Ivoire, the rising temperatures around the planet are increasing the strength of storms and the amount of flooding during the rainy season. Sea levels have risen, and salty seawater is invading freshwater marshes. Salt water is also seeping into underground sources of fresh water, damaging crops and spoiling drinking water.

Seawater has lapped away at beaches, endangering buildings in Abidjan and Grand-Bassam. Beach erosion has destroyed many homes and a lighthouse in the town of Grand-Lahou. Scientists report many of Côte d'Ivoire's beaches are eroding 3 to 6 feet (1 to 2 m) a year. This erosion is likely to increase in the future.

Western Côte d'Ivoire is more mountainous. The region is called the Eighteen Mountains. The land is green, and the temperatures are cooler than elsewhere in the country. The tallest peak in Côte d'Ivoire is Mount Nimba, which rises to 5,748 feet (1,752 meters) above sea level.

A man steers a dugout canoe called a pirogue near Grand-Lahou, where the Bandama River flows into the Gulf of Guinea.

Rivers and Lakes

Côte d'Ivoire has many rivers that flow north to south. There are four major river systems. From west to east, they are: Cavally, Sassandra, Bandama, and Comoé. Côte d'Ivoire's longest river, the Bandama, is joined by many rivers and streams and flows about 500 miles (800 kilometers) to the sea. The Cavally River rises near Mount Nimba. The river runs wild with rapids and waterfalls and forms most of the border with Liberia. It enters the Gulf of Guinea near Cape Palmas, a rocky peninsula at the Liberian border. Along the Cavally River, in a bamboo forest near the town of Man, is the stunning Zadépleu waterfall. Cool waters from the highlands cascade over tall rock cliffs creating a spectacular sight and a popular place to swim.

Most lakes have been created by dams. The largest, called Lake Kossou, covers 1,600 square miles (4,100 sq km) and is formed by one of the dams on the Bandama River.

Protecting Nature

Protecting and conserving natural resources has been a struggle in Côte d'Ivoire. The soil is rich, especially in the rain forest, and farmers and agriculture companies clear the forests to make room for farms and plantations. Historically, Côte d'Ivoire has had some of the most important tropical forests in the world, with thousands of native plants providing habitat for hundreds of different animal species. Many people want to preserve the country's remaining forests, and in some instances they have been successful.

Côte d'Ivoire has nine national parks and protected areas. Not all the parks have been kept safe from wildlife poachers

Many hikers travel to the spectacular Zadépleu waterfall for a refreshing swim.

(people who hunt illegally) and farmers who ignore park rules. Yet Ivoirians and international conservation groups are making progress. Comoé National Park is one of the largest protected areas in West Africa. It contains many types of landscapes, including savanna, rain forest, and wetlands along the Comoé River. Some of Africa's rarest animals live there, including chimpanzees and elephants.

Taï National Park, established in 1972, includes the largest untouched rain forest in West Africa. Many endangered species make their homes there, including the pygmy hippopotamus. In the Eighteen Mountains region, the Mount

Illegal logging has destroyed many towering trees in Côte d'Ivoire, even in forest reserves.

Nimba Strict Nature Reserve shares its boundaries with neighboring Guinea. The reserve supports many rare plants and threatened animal species.

Marahoué National Park has been damaged by illegal farming and poaching. As human activity increased, clashes erupted between people and the forest elephants living in the park. To solve the problem, the government and international wildlife organizations used helicopters and trucks to capture and transport the elephants to a new home in Assagny National Park (also spelled Azagny) near the Bandama River. Visitors to Assagny are allowed to walk only around the edges of the park.

Kob antelope are among the 135 species of mammals that live in the diverse habitats of Comoé National Park.

Climate

Côte d'Ivoire has a tropical climate, with warm temperatures year-round. February and March are the warmest months, with high temperatures in Abidjan averaging about 88 degrees

Ivoirians push a car through a flooded area near Abidjan. Floods are a common danger during the rainy season.

Fahrenheit (31 degrees Celsius). August is the coolest month, with temperatures dropping slightly to an average high of 80°F (27°C). Along the Gulf of Guinea and in the central regions, Côte d'Ivoire experiences four seasons. These regions have a long dry season from December to May and a long rainy season from May to July. From July to October is a short dry season followed by a short rainy season from October to November. During heavy storms, the coastal area, where most people live, is at risk from dangerous floods.

Northern Côte d'Ivoire experiences only two seasons: a rainy season from May to October and a dry season from November to April. Although the winter dry season brings relief from drenching rain and mud, it also brings hot, blustery harmattan winds. These winds form atop the sands of the Sahara Desert in North Africa. They howl across much of West Africa, tearing at rooftops, damaging crops, and lashing people and animals with sand and debris.

Urban Landscapes

Côte d'Ivoire's largest city, Abidjan, is home to about 4.4 million people. It was the capital of the country until 1983, and it remains the country's largest port and its economic center. The city has a good transportation system that links people with shops, supermarkets, department stores, banks, high-rise office towers, schools, colleges, museums, restaurants, galleries, and a busy commercial harbor.

Bouaké, Côte d'Ivoire's second-largest city with more than half a million residents, is a regional commercial center. The city features many French colonial style buildings, plus cafés, shops, banks, factories, a hospital, a university, and two soccer stadiums. Bouaké is known for its textile and food-processing industries.

Daloa is known for its rich greenery. The city

The Central Mosque is the oldest mosque in Bouaké, dating back to 1881.

has a population of about 245,000 people and is surrounded by plantations and lush forests. Daloa is a commercial hub for trade in coffee, cocoa, rubber, and palm oil. The city is home to people of many different African ethnic groups, as well as Western immigrants, giving the city a diverse culture.

Korhogo, located in the northern savanna, has a population of about 243,000 people. The city serves the region's farmers who bring their produce and livestock to market. In the 1930s, cotton plantations were established nearby, adding to Korhogo's commercial importance. The city's artists are renowned for their weaving, metalworking, and painting.

Abidjan has a bustling business district.

A Lush Landscape   **25**

CHAPTER 3

Tropical Splendor

CÔTE D'IVOIRE, LIKE ITS WEST AFRICAN NEIGHBORS, is home to a vast variety of plant and animal species. More than a thousand animal species and several thousand plant species live in the country. Parts of Côte d'Ivoire belong to the Guinean forest global biodiversity hotspot. A biodiversity hotspot is one of just a few areas in the world where large populations of diverse and rare species can be found living together.

Opposite: **The roloway monkey lives only in a small area of West Africa, including Côte d'Ivoire. It spends most of its time high in the treetops.**

Plant Life

Plants along the coast of Côte d'Ivoire grow amid a network of mangroves, swamps, marshes, rivers, and lagoons. Mangrove trees are particularly important to the health of animals and other plants in the area. Mangroves grow in shallow water near the sea. The water is brackish, a mixture of fresh and salt

A man drains latex, the material used to make natural rubber, from a rubber tree on a plantation in Côte d'Ivoire.

Danger to the Forest

At one time, nearly 80 percent of Côte d'Ivoire was covered in rain forest. Less than 20 percent of the rain forest remains today. The biggest threat to it is plantation farming that grows cocoa trees, palm trees, rubber, and coffee. These plants grow fastest in rain forest soil.

The farmers plant crops after cutting down or burning the trees. The soil is good for only a few years, leading the farmers to then burn more forest. Most of the remaining untouched rain forest lies within national parks and preserves, but even this is sometimes threatened.

water. Mangrove roots grow from the branches downward and form a tangled knot both above and below the surface of the water. Many plants and animals live among the roots. When the tide flows into the mangroves it brings food and nutrients for the plants and animals. When the tide ebbs, the mangrove roots capture mud and debris and eventually form land. The mangroves also protect land from being eroded by waves.

The rain forest is home to a variety of plant species, providing a rich habitat for many animals. Although much of the forest area has been transformed into agricultural fields and tree farms, the remaining rain forest is a wealth of vegetation. Hardwood trees that grow in the forest include white mahogany, teak, African oak, ironwood, rosewood, and limba. Côte d'Ivoire's hardwoods are prized around the world for making furniture, and the limba tree is also used for making guitars. Locally, limba is called the "malaria tree" because its bark is used to treat the disease. Other native trees found in the forest include kola nut, palm, coffee, and rubber. Together, they form a thick layer of leaves called the forest canopy. Some

A vast sugarcane plantation stretches across the land in northwestern Côte d'Ivoire. In many parts of the country, farms have replaced forests.

Kola Nuts

The kola nut tree grows in southern Côte d'Ivoire. The tree produces large white pods that contain edible nuts. The nuts are chewed, eaten whole, boiled, or mashed into powder and mixed with a liquid to make a drink. They are also used as a cooking spice and in traditional medicines to treat ailments as varied as headaches, stomachaches, asthma, and whooping cough. The kola nut contains caffeine, and many people, especially laborers, chew the nut for energy throughout the day.

In 1886, a pharmacist in the United States made a mixture of kola nuts, coca, sugar, coloring, and carbonated water. Doing so, he created a soft drink he named Coca-Cola. Kola nuts are no longer part of the Coca-Cola recipe, but the tree is grown commercially in Côte d'Ivoire and kola nuts are sold around the world.

In Cote d'Ivoire, the kola nut is considered sacred. It is shared during rituals such as naming ceremonies and weddings.

trees, such as the kapok tree, are called emergent trees because they grow taller than the canopy. Some of them can grow to 250 feet (75 m). Thick vines and lianas (vine-like plants that send their roots into trees) begin at the forest floor and grow upward to reach sunlight. The rain forest canopy blocks out light below, so the forest floor is somewhat bare of plants. Plants that grow beneath the canopy are orchids, lichens, mosses, and bromeliads. Bromeliads are colorful plants that store water for long periods of time, such as wild pineapple.

Hundreds of species of grasses, shrubs, and trees grow in the savanna. Grasses include red oat grass, star grass, lemongrass, and elephant grass, which grows along riverbanks in clumps up to 10 feet (3 m) tall. The savanna's flowering bushes include hibiscus, frangipani, bougainvillea, and okra. Bushes and shrubs cover much of the savanna, while trees usually grow solo. There are several species of savanna trees. The acacia produces a sticky sap used to treat skin irritations and sore throats. The tall whistling thorn tree attracts stinging ants. The ants bore holes in the tree, and when the wind blows across the holes it produces a loud whistle. The West African karité tree bears a nut that produces shea butter, a popular oil used in cooking and skin creams. The mighty baobab tree lives in the drier parts of the savanna and can survive for thousands of years. A baobab can grow up to 80 feet (25 m) high and has an enormous trunk that holds water throughout the dry season. The baobab is sacred to people and is often called the Tree of Life.

The Eighteen Mountains region surrounding Mount Nimba contains hundreds of species of plants, many of them rare. Trees found at lower elevations include thick tropical forests of palm, bamboo, ficus, and ebony. Among the trees grow flowering plants such as lobelia, orchid, gladiola, and spider plant. Mists cover the mountaintops where smaller plants grow, including mosses, lichens, herbs, and giant ferns.

Creatures of the Water

Some of the most common species of fish that live in the rivers of Côte d'Ivoire include carp, flounder, perch, catfish, and tilapia. These are all important foods for people. Some smaller fish that live in the rivers are familiar to people by way of aquariums, such as lampreys, tetras, damselfish, and the rare

A Useful Flower

One of the most beautiful flowers in Côte d'Ivoire is the lantana, which belongs to the verbena family. The plant, which grows in most soils, is a low-growing shrub that produces clusters of flowers and spreads rapidly. Flowers bloom all year and bloom in many colors, including pink, red, yellow, purple, blue, and white. In Côte d'Ivoire, the leaves are used in herbal medicines to treat skin irritations, chicken pox, measles, and asthma.

Lantana produces a mix of colors within a single cluster of flowers.

elephant nose fish. Endangered fish from Côte d'Ivoire include the walking catfish, which can breathe air and use its fins to walk short distances on land.

Along the coast, crabs, shrimp, lobsters, oysters, and clams live in lagoons and mangroves. Many young fish such as grouper, ladyfish, and snapper spawn in shallow water and feed in the mangroves, where the tangle of roots gives them protection from predators. Small fish such as herring and young shad are at the bottom of the food chain and provide food for larger fish such as pompano, barracuda, salmon, pike, tiger fish, tarpon, mackerel, and sawfish. Other sea-dwelling animals include rays, eels, sea snakes, sharks, and marine mammals. Many of the marine mammals are threatened or endangered, including the humpback whale, the Southern right whale, and the rare Atlantic humpback dolphin. Another marine mammal, the manatee, is large and slow-moving. Manatees live in warm, shallow water and feed on seagrasses and algae. Although manatees live in the ocean, they are related to elephants and not whales.

Creatures of the Air

A multitude of colorful butterflies, moths, and birds can be found throughout Côte d'Ivoire. Butterflies and moths feed on the flowers of trees, shrubs, plants, and bushes.

Bird experts have observed at least 730 species of birds living in Côte d'Ivoire. Some live in Côte d'Ivoire year-round, while others stop to feed while migrating to and from other

One of the hundreds of bird species found in Côte d'Ivoire is the black-crowned crane, an elegant bird that is about 3 feet (1 m) from head to tail.

Tropical Splendor   33

The National Bird

The national bird of Côte d'Ivoire is the white-cheeked turaco, a striking bird with blue-black feathers, white cheeks, crimson feathers under its wings, and a bright orange bill. It has a long tail to help it balance. Turacos eat mainly forest fruits and plants. During mating season, the birds chase each other from tree to tree and make loud calls that sound like monkey calls. When a turaco senses danger, it perches very still and flies away at the last moment.

regions. Still others spend the winter in Côte d'Ivoire to avoid cold temperatures elsewhere.

Along the coast are flocks of gulls, terns, petrels, and pelicans, as well as plovers, oystercatchers, and sandpipers. The endangered rufous fishing owl lives nowhere else in the world but on the coast of Côte d'Ivoire. Coastal lagoons and wetlands provide a bounty of plants, worms, and food fish that attract ospreys, ducks, and geese. The wetlands are also home to many wading birds, including herons, egrets, flamingos, and storks.

Most rain forest birds live in the canopy, eating fruit, seeds, nuts, or insects. The forests are home to brilliantly colored birds such as the fire-bellied woodpecker, crested guinea fowl, and the blue-whiskered bee-eater. Some birds live in the emergent trees above the rain forest canopy. These include species of hummingbirds, parrots, parakeets, lovebirds, and macaws.

Many species of birds make the savanna their home, including the quail, sparrow, finch, vulture, starling, fly-catcher, and weaver. The male weaverbird is a persistent nest builder. He weaves an intricate nest of twigs and grasses and suspends it from a bare hanging branch. However, the female weaverbird must approve the construction before she will lay her eggs. If she disapproves, she will rip the nest apart and the male weaverbird has to start again.

Raptors, or birds of prey, live throughout Côte d'Ivoire. One of the most common is the Congo serpent eagle, whose loud calls can be heard over great distances. The largest raptor in Côte d'Ivoire is the crowned eagle, which preys on monkeys.

Reptiles

Although many reptiles in Côte d'Ivoire are threatened, there remain about 125 species. Many chameleons live in the savanna. They range in size from 2 inches to 2 feet (5 to 60 centimeters). The nation is also home to land tortoises such as the African mud turtle and the rain forest–dwelling rosy

hingeback tortoise. Many of the world's most endangered sea turtles come ashore to lay their eggs on Ivoirian beaches, including olive ridley, leatherback, and hawksbill turtles.

Côte d'Ivoire was once home to many Nile and West African crocodiles, but they have been hunted to near extinction. Snakes are common everywhere in the country. Many are harmless to humans. Even the 12-foot (4 m) rock python does not pose a threat to people. However, an attack by a venomous snake such as a green mamba, puff adder, Gaboon viper, or spitting cobra is usually lethal.

Mammals

As with plants and other animals, mammals have seen their habitats decrease as forests and grasslands have been taken over by farms. Many elephants once roamed the forests of

Côte d'Ivoire, but today the country's elephant population has dwindled to just a few hundred. Most of them live in Taï and Assagny National Parks. The African forest elephant on average grows to 8 feet (2.5 m) in height. The elephants' trunks contain more than one hundred thousand muscles. They use their trunks to drink, gather food, bathe, communicate, attack, and defend. Other herbivores in Côte d'Ivoire are

Forest elephants are herbivores, feeding on grasses, leaves, bark, and fruit.

Hippopotamuses feed mostly on plants, but they are the most dangerous large animal in Africa. Hippos kill about three thousand people a year, many of whom strayed near their young.

ten antelope species, including two of the world's rarest—the Jentink's duiker and the striped zebra duiker.

The hippopotamus is Côte d'Ivoire's second-largest animal after the elephant. Males can weigh as much as 7,000 pounds (3,200 kilograms). The rare pygmy hippopotamus can also be found in Côte d'Ivoire, deep in the wild wetlands of Taï National Park. Hippopotamuses are sensitive to the sun, so they stay caked in mud or underwater throughout the day. When night falls, hippopotamuses come onto land to graze

on grass. Despite having an enormous mouth and giant canine teeth, the hippopotamus eats mostly plants.

The carnivorous, or meat-eating, mammals of Côte d'Ivoire include mongooses, hyenas, jackals, and wild cats. Lions live mostly in the savanna, where they hunt in small groups. They hunt when it gets dark, preying on wild hogs, antelopes, and hippopotamuses, and domestic animals such as goats and cattle. Leopards also attack at night, preying on antelopes, monkeys, and wild pigs. Other wild cats that live in Côte d'Ivoire include servals, civets, and the African golden cat.

A huge variety of animals live in the rain forest. The sloth, a relative of the anteater, lives in the emergent layer. It is the world's slowest animal, so slow that moss grows on its back. One of the fastest animals in the rain forest is the spider monkey, which swings from branch to branch. Other monkeys that live in Côte d'Ivoire include the mona, colobus, mangabey, and patas.

The chimpanzee is the closest animal relative to humans. The African chimpanzee once thrived in Côte d'Ivoire and other parts of West Africa, but now is an endangered species. Some of the last remaining chimpanzees live in Comoé and Taï National Parks. Their habitat is closely protected. Scientists studying the Taï chimpanzees discovered that they make tools such as hammers and brushes out of sticks, roots, and stones. Taï National Park and other nature preserves are beginning to allow some visitors into the protected areas. Officials hope that income from tourists will help protect and expand Côte d'Ivoire's wild habitats and valuable plants and animals.

CHAPTER 4

Paths Through Time

I T IS UNCLEAR WHEN THE EARLIEST CIVILIZATIONS existed in Côte d'Ivoire. Scientists have discovered weapons, tools, and cooking pots dating from 4500 to 2000 BCE. However, many say other civilizations might have been present as early as 15,000 to 10,000 BCE. These scientists point out that the earliest people may have settled in the rain forest where skeletons and the remains of their civilization decomposed in the wet, fertile soil.

Opposite: **A Senufo mask from northern Côte d'Ivoire**

First Settlers

Many of the ethnic groups in Côte d'Ivoire migrated from other areas of West Africa. It is believed that before these migrants arrived, the ancient Gagu people were the first to settle in the region, but little is known about them. The first written record of West African civilizations came from Berber

It took about forty days for Berber traders to travel across the Sahara to the kingdoms of West Africa.

The Introduction of Islam

When Berber traders came to West Africa to trade with the Kingdom of Ghana, they introduced the teachings of Islam and the Arabic language. In the thirteenth century, the Malinke people, rulers of the Mali Empire, spread Islam through the savanna region of what is now Côte d'Ivoire. Traders began learning Arabic, the language of Islam, because it was used as a common business language. Later, in the eighteenth century, the Dyula people spread the religion farther. When Malinke Samory Touré founded his Wassoulou Empire in the nineteenth century, he and his Malinke followers introduced Islam southward.

traders in the eighth century CE. The Berber people were nomads who lived in North Africa and traded with Arab merchants. They brought Arab goods such as spices and salt across the Sahara Desert to trade with people in western Africa. Their first important West African trading partner was the Kingdom of Ghana, which was ruled by the Soninke people. The Soninke were artful traders. In their search for more gold and ivory to trade to the Berbers, some Soninke people began hunting for ivory and mining gold in what is now Côte d'Ivoire. By the twelfth century, the Ghana Empire had fallen.

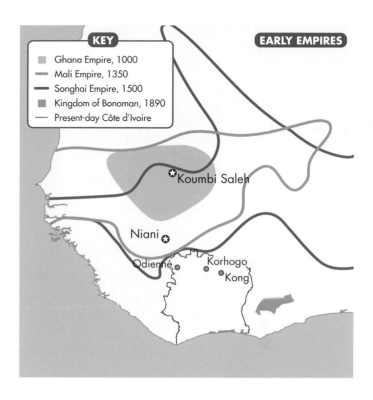

In the twelfth century, members of the Senufo ethnic group migrated to Côte d'Ivoire from Mali. They established the agricultural chiefdom of Korhogo. Also at that time, Mande-speaking groups established a city and trading center in Kong, in northern Côte d'Ivoire. They were successful traders and joined with some Senufo people to turn Kong into a major hub for the exchange of salt and cloth for kola nuts, dates, gold, and enslaved people.

Mali became the next major trading center. The Mali Empire spread across West Africa, becoming one of the most advanced civilizations in the world. Its major cities contained libraries and universities. The Mali Empire expanded into northwestern Côte d'Ivoire, where the Malians established the city of Odienné in the fourteenth century. Odienné became a center for agriculture and raising livestock.

After the fall of the Ghana Empire, people from the Akan ethnic group established a new trading center, called the Kingdom of Bonoman. Akan traders migrated in large numbers across West Africa. In eastern Côte d'Ivoire, they found gold, ivory, and fertile farmland. Today, Akan people are the majority ethnic group in Côte d'Ivoire.

Rise and Fall

The kingdoms of West Africa were based on peaceful trade between merchants. There was little reason for conflict. But as empires and kingdoms grew wealthier and more powerful, they used violence to compete for territory and resources.

The Mali Empire began to crumble late in the fourteenth century. It was conquered by members of the Songhai ethnic group, who also took over Odienné. When the Songhai Empire was conquered in the sixteenth century, many people fled south of Odienné into the forest. The Kong chiefdom was conquered by the Dyula people. They ruled the Kong kingdom until 1898.

As fortunes rose and fell in other parts of West Africa, many groups subdivided and migrated into Côte d'Ivoire. In the region that is now Ghana, the Asante, a group also belonging to the Akan ethnic group, rose to power. They controlled much of the trade between the coast and other West African groups. Not all Akan groups wanted to belong to the Asante Empire, and several groups fled to the region that is now Côte d'Ivoire. These included the Abron, the Baoulé, and the Anyi peoples.

Over centuries of migration, few groups had settled in the rain forest. The thick vegetation turned back merchants, traders, and farmers. Consequently, only north and central Côte d'Ivoire were settled. But as battles continued to erupt

The Legend of Queen Abla Pokou

In the eighteenth century, at the height of power of the Asante Empire, the people were left without a ruler. The king had died, and suddenly and mysteriously, two heirs also lost their lives. Abla Pokou, who was in line for the throne, was also threatened. She fled with a group of loyalists. After walking for several days, they reached the Comoé River, in what is now the eastern part of Côte d'Ivoire. The river was impassable and their enemies were not far behind.

Queen Abla Pokou sought advice from the group's wise man who told her they must make an offering to the river to make it passable. When offerings of gold and cattle did not calm the raging water, Abla Pokou chose to sacrifice her infant son. Legend has it that after she placed her son in the river, the river calmed and the people crossed to safety. When sacrificing her son, the queen had cried out "Ba Ouli!" which means "the child is dead." Baoulé became the name of one of Côte d'Ivoire's largest and most influential ethnic groups.

between rival groups, the rain forest in southern Côte d'Ivoire offered protection to fleeing groups.

Some newcomers to the forest encountered members of the Kru ethnic group, who, as fishers and sailors, had already settled along the coasts of what is now Liberia and Côte

Hundreds of captives were packed belowdecks on slave ships. Each person was given space just 16 inches (41 cm) wide and 3 feet (90 cm) high for the journey, which took months.

d'Ivoire. By the fifteenth century, Côte d'Ivoire had settlements extending from the coast, through the rain forest, along the rivers, and into the West African inland empires.

Trade Turns Ugly

More than sixty ethnic groups live in Côte d'Ivoire, and many settled more than two hundred years ago. Groups established villages, states, chiefdoms, and kingdoms. Trade continued between farmers, artisans, gold miners, hunters, and fishers. When conflicts broke out, sometimes one group enslaved people from other groups. The enslaved people, too, were traded.

The people of Côte d'Ivoire met their first non-Africans in the fifteenth century. Portuguese merchants sailed along the coast of West Africa, coming ashore in the region in 1482. The Portuguese developed peaceful trade relationships with most African leaders. In Côte d'Ivoire, the Portuguese traded cloth and beads for gold and ivory. Elephant ivory was prized by wealthy Europeans. The material is soft enough to carve intricate patterns into and was used for decorations, jewelry, and musical instruments.

Dutch, British, and French merchants followed the Portuguese. With them came the demand for more ivory. Ivoirian hunters were forced inland in search of elephants. The farther they went, the more difficult it was to transport the ivory back to the traders' ships. Hunters began enslaving laborers to do the work. Other African traders did the same, enslaving workers to mine for gold and to plant and harvest crops. The Europeans began sending enslaved workers to their new plantations in the Americas. The slave trade lasted from the fifteenth century until 1870. European merchants who had once come for spices and treasure now came for enslaved human labor. African leaders who had once traded their natural resources now traded humans. They no longer wanted luxury goods from Europe. Instead, they wanted guns to use in capturing and enslaving more people. It was a vicious cycle.

Côte d'Ivoire suffered somewhat less than other West

African countries. By the 1700s, the elephant population had been nearly destroyed, so Côte d'Ivoire no longer had a luxury item to trade. Nor did it have a natural harbor where slave-trading ships could anchor.

Enter the French

French missionaries established their first outpost in the Côte d'Ivoire region at Assinie on the Ébrié Lagoon in 1637. The French who followed did not focus as much on the slave trade as other Europeans did. Rather, they sought resources such

French troops began occupying posts along Ébrié Lagoon in the nineteenth century.

as lumber and groundnuts, which are similar to peanuts. They signed several treaties with local leaders, promising to pay a fee in exchange for use of the land and raw materials. Not all the leaders were willing to sign treaties. Many agreed only after the French used military force.

France began building an empire in the mid-1800s. In 1884, the French signed treaties placing the Assinie and nearby Grand-Bassam regions under French protection. Explorers, missionary priests, traders, and soldiers then

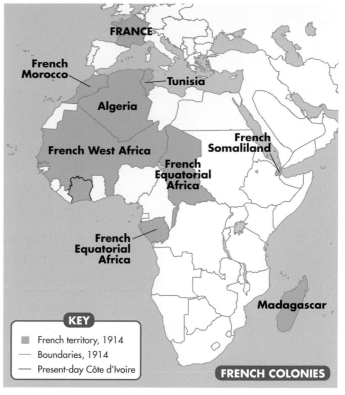

FRANCE

French Morocco

Tunisia

Algeria

French West Africa

French Somaliland

French Equatorial Africa

French Equatorial Africa

Madagascar

KEY

■ French territory, 1914
— Boundaries, 1914
— Present-day Côte d'Ivoire

FRENCH COLONIES

spread throughout the country. European powers were actively claiming territories in Asia and Africa. The French were determined to expand their influence beyond the borders of France, too. In Africa as well as in Asia, the French expanded trade and exploited sources of raw materials. They established plantations for growing crops such as cotton and coffee. The French also wanted to spread their culture across the globe. They believed their language, art, music, and literature were superior to others.

France also had political reasons to reinforce its control in Africa. Around the world, the French and the British were vying for power. To fend off the British, France built naval bases along the Ébrié Lagoon and sent its military inland.

In February 1885, European powers with interests in Africa held a conference. France, Germany, Portugal, and Britain met to discuss dividing their claims in West Africa. In 1889, the British recognized France's control over Côte d'Ivoire and other parts of West Africa.

Colonial Côte d'Ivoire

Louis-Gustave Binger, a French naval captain, explored and mapped Côte d'Ivoire from the coast to the interior. He wrote books about his explorations and learned to speak a few local languages. When Côte d'Ivoire was named a colony in 1893, Binger was appointed its first governor.

In West Africa, the French set up a strict central government instead of working with local leaders. The French justice system conflicted with West African systems. Traditionally, village chiefs or councils judged people who disobeyed a law or mistreated another person. Usually the offender was ordered to apologize and make amends to the community. Under French rule, people were sent to prison.

France's main goal in West Africa was to produce and export agricultural products and natural resources. With this in mind, the French government encouraged citizens to settle in Côte d'Ivoire. Mining and logging companies hired African laborers and French settlers to oversee operations. The government provided money, but large international companies built transportation systems to deliver goods to port. French plantations were very profitable. They grew coffee, cocoa, bananas, oil palms, and rubber trees. Planters paid workers

Samory Touré fought the French for more than a decade.

Rebel Leader

A man named Samory Touré, a member of the Malinke ethnic group, founded the Wassoulou Empire. He was born around 1830 in the Wassoulou River Valley. His father was a trader, and Touré followed in his footsteps. But one day his mother was captured in a raid by a neighboring king. Touré could not afford his mother's ransom, so he traded her freedom for his and joined the king's army, where he learned military tactics and leadership skills.

Touré resented the growing influence of the French in West Africa. He ventured across the region uniting villagers and recruiting soldiers for his army, which grew to thirty thousand men. Touré took over most of northern Côte d'Ivoire between 1893 and 1898 and established a new capital in the city of Kong. For eighteen years, he resisted and frustrated the colonial French army. He was finally captured one morning while praying outside his home. He was exiled, and died in 1900.

very little, some so little that it was more like slavery than employment. They also practiced forced labor. If there were not enough people to get the work done on one plantation, people living in other villages were told to leave home and go where their labor was needed.

Changes in Society

The French brought political and economic change to Côte d'Ivoire. France declared that French was the colony's official language and people were told to accept France's laws and customs. Officially, the people were called subjects of France, not citizens. French Africans could not vote or have representatives in government. French officials appointed local leaders who were allies and dismissed or demoted traditional leaders. In 1900, a tax was levied on each adult. Those who were unable to pay were forced to work in the mines, building

Nearly half a million African troops fought for France in World War I, most of them in Europe.

roads, or on plantations. Men were expected to serve in the military. The tax, forced labor, low pay, and lack of the rights of citizenship increasingly angered the Africans.

The French also introduced social change. Catholic missionaries established churches, schools, and libraries. Some Ivoirians, mostly the sons of wealthy farmers and officials, attended high school and universities in France. Many who knew French had successful careers in business and government. They enjoyed many privileges given to white settlers, such as exemption from military service. However, the French maintained two sets of laws, one for whites and another for Africans.

Wars and Independence

In 1914, World War I began in Europe. France was in the middle of the war and called upon its colonies to supply troops. As many as 150,000 Ivoirian soldiers were killed in the war. The people of Côte d'Ivoire, including the wealthy and educated class, demanded to know why they were expected to fight for a distant country that denied them basic rights.

In the years after World War I ended, in 1918, Côte d'Ivoire's agricultural production increased and its economy grew. But life was still difficult for many Ivoirian farmers. The French plantation owners got higher prices and paid their workers far less than African farmers did.

In 1939, World War II began in Europe, as Nazi Germany began invading neighboring countries. The following year, Germany invaded France. Exports from Côte d'Ivoire dropped drastically, and the country's economy nearly collapsed.

Again, France expected Ivoirians to contribute to their war effort. More workers were forced into labor, and farms were told to increase production.

Germany installed a Nazi government in France, called the Vichy government. The rulers of French West Africa pledged loyalty to the Vichy government, and many Nazis moved to Côte d'Ivoire. The Nazis, who held racist views, were deeply destructive to Côte d'Ivoire's society and economy. They treated the Africans cruelly, forcing them to work harder and longer for less pay.

As the war continued, a group of Ivoirian students and

Ivoirian workers at a cotton factory. Industry grew in Côte d'Ivoire in the mid-twentieth century.

The Old One

Félix Houphouët-Boigny was born to a well-to-do Baoulé family in 1905. He was educated in French boarding schools and was trained as a doctor. He became deeply involved in the rights of Ivoirians; in particular he fought tirelessly against forced labor.

After Houphouët-Boigny became the Ivoirian representative in the French Parliament in 1945, he spoke up for the rights of all French West Africans. He helped write Côte d'Ivoire's first constitution and led the drive for independence. Houphouët-Boigny fought to abolish racism and discrimination in his country and was the first Catholic public figure in Côte d'Ivoire to marry a Muslim. Elected president in 1960, he served until his death in 1993. Ivoirians affectionately refer to him as Le Vieux, which means the Old One.

Félix Houphouët-Boigny was a major political figure in Côte d'Ivoire for more than four decades.

intellectuals gathered to discuss the mistreatment of Ivoirians by white colonialists. In 1944, a Baoulé farmer and local official named Félix Houphouët-Boigny founded the African Agricultural Union (SAA) to protect the rights of Ivoirian farmers from the unfair advantage taken by white farmers. In

Abidjan was a thriving city in the mid-twentieth century.

just a short time, the union had twenty thousand members.

The Vichy government was removed from power in 1943. France recognized that the SAA and the movement toward equality were getting stronger. In 1944, France held a conference in Brazzaville, Republic of the Congo, to discuss reforms in its colonies. France agreed to give Côte d'Ivoire and colonies in West Africa more independence. They were granted the right to hold elections for a representative to the French Parliament.

In 1945, Houphouët-Boigny became the first Ivoirian representative to the French Parliament. Once in Paris, he became the leader of two new political movements—the Democratic Party of Côte d'Ivoire (PDCI) and the African Democratic Rally (RDA). The groups were a mix of communists, socialists, and liberals from French West Africa. The

French government quickly imprisoned many members of the PDCI and RDA. Large protests erupted.

In 1958, the French government and many West African leaders agreed to semi-independence. Africans would be allowed to draft their own constitutions and elect representatives to local governments. France retained control of the military and banking and finance. However, on August 7, 1960, Côte d'Ivoire formally declared itself independent from France. Later that year, Houphouët-Boigny was elected Côte d'Ivoire's first president.

In 1961, Félix Houphouët-Boigny (right) and Senegalese president Léopold Senghor (left) celebrate the first anniversary of Ivoirian independence. Senegal had also become independent the previous year.

Modernization

Under President Houphouët-Boigny, Côte d'Ivoire experienced an economic boom. The government spent money improving roads and other infrastructure, which also provided many people with jobs. Farming also expanded. In the 1960s, Côte d'Ivoire became the world's largest exporter of palm oil and pineapples. In another decade it would become the world's largest producer of cocoa. As foreign engineers and technical workers were hired to modernize roads, railways, and airports, and to build hotels, universities, office buildings, and housing for the wealthy, fewer good jobs remained for Ivoirians.

Henri Konan Bédié served as ambassador to the United States, as finance minister, and as a member of the National Assembly before becoming president.

Houphouët-Boigny also made a number of unpopular choices that angered citizens. He encouraged migrant workers from Mali, Ghana, and Burkina Faso to work on the ever-expanding plantations. He allowed only one political party and handpicked the people for important government positions. He also favored people from the majority ethnic groups. By the late 1960s, many people protested Houphouët-Boigny's rule, but most were silenced and some were arrested. Some people from minority ethnic groups tried to secede from the country. The president wanted to restore calm. He visited villages around the country and asked what he could do to improve the lives of the people.

War and Strife

In the 1970s, economic trouble arose. The price for coffee and cocoa dropped by more than half. Many Ivoirians were out of work. Crime increased. With fewer jobs, foreign workers and Ivoirians became more hostile toward each other. Unrest continued until Houphouët-Boigny's death in 1993. He was succeeded by Henri Konan Bédié, the president of the National Assembly, who then ran in the 1995 presidential election unopposed. During Bédié's term, corruption, poverty, and unemployment continued to plague the nation. In 1999, military officers presented him with a list of demands. Rather than negotiate, President Bédié took a hard line. He was deposed and forced to leave the country.

The military ruled for one year, until a bitter election was won by Laurent Gbagbo, a liberal socialist. He also held the opinion that foreign migrant workers took jobs away from native Ivoirians. Additionally, he declared that foreign companies and the rich did even greater damage to the Ivoirian economy. Although Gbagbo ousted some foreign companies and workers, the economy worsened.

Many members of northern ethnic groups were dissatisfied with the treatment they received from the government. In 2002, a large group of Ivoirian rebel soldiers descended on the country's major cities and gained control of most of northern Côte d'Ivoire. This was the beginning of Côte d'Ivoire's first civil war. The French and the United Nations (UN) sent three thousand peacekeeping troops to prevent the rebel soldiers from taking over Abidjan. Throughout 2002 and 2003, French troops and the rebel soldiers fought in a number of skirmishes. The nation became politically split between north and south. More UN peacekeepers arrived. People on both sides protested, and in 2004, five hundred demonstrators were shot and killed. Later that year, the government bombed a French military post, and French soldiers retaliated. Assaults on both sides continued until a settlement was reached in 2007.

In 2010, President Gbagbo agreed to hold elections. He lost the election, but he and his supporters did not concede. Instead, intense fighting broke out between Gbagbo's supporters and those of the newly elected president, Alassane Ouattara, an economist and former prime minister. This was the beginning of Côte d'Ivoire's second civil war. Innocent people were murdered and buried in mass graves. Protesters were gunned down, and more than 450,000 Ivoirians fled

overseas. In 2011, northern rebels overtook Abidjan. Gbagbo was taken into custody and accused by the International Criminal Court of war crimes. The second civil war was over.

Recovery

President Ouattara was reelected in 2015. He has forged new relationships with foreign countries and the economy is growing. Yet, while income is improving rapidly for corporations and wealthy Ivoirians, nearly half of the country's citizens live in poverty. Additionally, tension and distrust still exist between the groups that opposed each other in the last civil war. Despite unsteady progress, there has been remarkable growth in Côte d'Ivoire. However, the nation's present and future challenges are to build peace between ethnic groups and achieve greater social and economic equality.

CHAPTER 5

Governing the Republic

THE GOVERNMENT OF CÔTE D'IVOIRE TODAY BEARS little resemblance to its past governments. The country was settled slowly and by different ethnic groups with different customs and ideals. As each group migrated, they formed communities and governments of their own. Some of the groups were part of larger kingdoms and empires, while others settled in villages led by local or regional leaders. Not until the French arrived in Côte d'Ivoire did the country establish a central government.

France colonized Côte d'Ivoire in the nineteenth century and established a government based on the French constitution. In 1960, Côte d'Ivoire became independent and adopted a new constitution. The constitution was rewritten in 2000 and 2016. The latest constitution guarantees the right to assemble, freedom of speech, freedom of religion, and freedom

Opposite: **A woman casts a vote at a polling station in Abidjan. In Côte d'Ivoire, people must be at least eighteen years old to vote.**

of the press. It calls for free compulsory education and bans discrimination based on race, religion, gender, or disability.

National Government of Côte d'Ivoire

Executive Branch
President
Vice President
Prime Minister
Council of Ministers

Legislative Branch
Senate | National Assembly

Judicial Branch
Council of Magistracy
Supreme Court
Court of Cassation | Council of State
Courts of Appeals
Courts of First Instance

The Executive Branch

Côte d'Ivoire's constitution describes three branches of government: executive, legislative, and judicial. The executive branch is led by the president, a vice president, and

The National Flag

The flag of Côte d'Ivoire contains three vertical bands of color. From left to right the colors are orange, white, and green. Orange symbolizes national growth, white represents peace and unity, and green represents a bright future. Unofficially, the orange is said to represent the savanna of the north, white is for the nation's rivers, and green symbolizes the southern rain forests.

The flag of Côte d'Ivoire was adopted in 1959.

the government. The president is the head of state. He or she is elected for a five-year term and can be reelected only once. In order to be a candidate for office, the president must have a mother or father who was a native-born Ivoirian. The president's responsibilities include setting national policies, proposing laws, acting as head of the armed forces, and ensuring the enforcement of laws and court decisions. The president appoints the vice president, the prime minister, ministers, and the justices of the Supreme Court as well as many high-ranking administrators.

The office of the vice president was newly created in the constitution of 2016. The vice president is responsible for taking over the duties of the president if the president is out of the country.

The prime minister is the head of government and is responsible for organizing and overseeing government decisions and the legislature. He or she is also responsible for taking over duties of the president if both the president and the vice president are out of the country. The prime minister leads the Council of Ministers, a group of officials who are in charge of different subjects central to the government and country, such as finance, defense, health, education, mining, fisheries, human rights, social services, and trade.

The Legislative Branch

The legislative branch of Côte d'Ivoire is a parliament with two houses, the National Assembly and the Senate. The members of the National Assembly are called deputies. In 2017, there were 255 deputies, but this number can change as the population changes. The Senate has 120 seats. Two-thirds of senators are elected by regional councils. The president appoints the other

Members of the National Assembly examine a bill.

Students march in a parade celebrating Ivoirian independence.

The National Anthem

Although Abidjan is no longer the capital of Côte d'Ivoire, the national anthem is called "L'Abidjanaise" ("The Song of Abidjan"). The words are by Mathieu Ekra and Joachim Bony, and the music is by Pierre-Marie Coty and Pierre-Michel Pango. The song was adopted in 1960, the year the country became independent.

French lyrics

Salut Ô terre d'espérance;
Pays de l'hospitalité.
Tes légions remplies de vaillance
Ont relevé ta dignité.
Tes fils, chère Côte d'Ivoire,
Fiers artisans de ta grandeur,
Tous rassemblés pour ta gloire
Te bâtiront dans le bonheur.

Fiers Ivoiriens, le pays nous appelle.
Si nous avons dans la paix ramené la
*   liberté,*
Notre devoir sera d'être un modèle
De l'espérance promise à l'humanité,
En forgeant, unie dans la foi nouvelle,
La patrie de la vraie fraternité.

English translation

We salute you, O land of hope,
Country of hospitality;
Thy full gallant legions
Have restored thy dignity.
Beloved Côte d'Ivoire, thy sons,
Proud builders of thy greatness,
All gathered together for thy glory,
In joy will we construct thee.

Proud Ivoirians, the country calls us.
If we have brought back liberty peacefully,
It will be our duty to be an example
Of the hope promised to humanity,
In building, united in the new faith
The homeland of true brotherhood.

one-third. All members of parliament serve five-year terms. The responsibility of parliament is to pass laws and approve taxes. Either house can propose a bill, and both houses must agree to pass it into law.

Many ethnic communities and villages maintain traditional governments. They have a chief or a king, whose authority is inherited. The chiefs rely on councils in their decision making.

A chief in Grand-Jacques, in southern Côte d'Ivoire

The Judicial Branch

The judicial branch of government consists of its courts, which interpret and apply laws. The court system in Côte d'Ivoire is presided over by the Council of Magistracy. The council is made up of retired judges who are appointed by the president. The Council of Magistracy examines court rulings and recommends persons for judgeships.

The Supreme Court of Côte d'Ivoire has two parts—the Court of Cassation and the Council of State. The Court of Cassation is the nation's highest court and makes final decisions about cases appealed from lower courts. The Council of State is the highest court for administration decisions, such as lawsuits.

The constitution of 2016 created the National Chamber of Kings and Traditional Chiefs to protect traditional customs and to recommend peaceful solutions to disputes within villages and between communities.

A Look at the Capital

Abidjan was the original capital city of Côte d'Ivoire. It is still the nation's acting capital, although it is no longer the official one. Most government organizations and foreign embassies remain headquartered in Abidjan.

In 1983, the official capital of Côte d'Ivoire was moved to a small village in the central part of the country that was the birthplace of the nation's first president, Félix Houphouët-Boigny. He wanted to build a capital city from the ground up. He named it Yamoussoukro, in honor of his aunt Yamoussou.

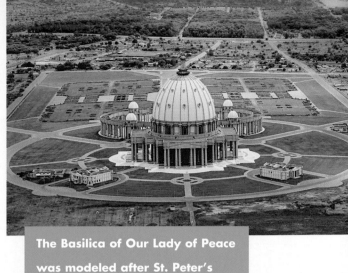

The Basilica of Our Lady of Peace was modeled after St. Peter's Basilica in Rome, Italy.

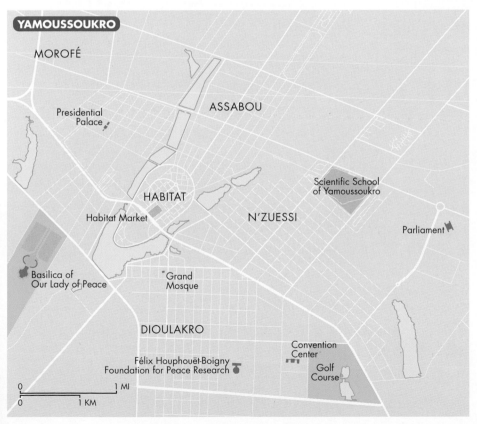

YAMOUSSOUKRO

MOROFÉ

Presidential Palace

ASSABOU

HABITAT

Habitat Market

Scientific School of Yamoussoukro

N'ZUESSI

Parliament

Basilica of Our Lady of Peace

Grand Mosque

DIOULAKRO

Félix Houphouët-Boigny Foundation for Peace Research

Convention Center

Golf Course

0   1 MI
0   1 KM

Today, Yamoussoukro is home to more than two hundred thousand people. It is a city of wide boulevards. Forestry, fishing, and perfume are all important to the economy. Aside from government buildings, notable structures include an ornate hotel, a conference center devoted to peace, and one of the world's largest Catholic churches. Houphouët-Boigny ordered the construction of the Basilica of Our Lady of Peace, which took thirteen years to complete. The church can hold eighteen thousand people.

CHAPTER 6

On the Rise

CÔTE D'IVOIRE HAS ONE OF THE FASTEST-GROWING economies in the world. Since the end of its second civil war, the nation's government has worked hard to build the economy, provide jobs, and gain the trust of world trading partners. Agriculture has always been the most important part of the economy. It takes two forms, farming for food and farming for cash crops. Agriculture employs nearly 70 percent of the population. But other industries are growing and adding to the economy.

Agriculture

Côte d'Ivoire's soils are extremely fertile, even in the drier parts of the savanna. The Kru people in the southwest grow yams, a staple in Côte d'Ivoire, as well as corn, peanuts, cassava, and plantains. They also collect kola and oil palm nuts.

Opposite: **Professional laundry washers clean other people's laundry in a creek in the Adjamé neighborhood of Abidjan. Many people have moved from the country to the city in recent years, settling in working-class neighborhoods such as Adjamé.**

Many farmers in southeastern Côte d'Ivoire grow pineapples. Bouaké is a major rice-producing region. The Senufo people in northern Côte d'Ivoire grow millet, sorghum, corn, rice, and yams. They also grow bananas, manioc, and raise farm animals. Most livestock are raised in the north. Ranchers raise chickens, goats, sheep, cattle, and hogs.

Several fish farms have been established along the rivers near Korhogo and Bouaké. Fishing fleets based in Abidjan catch more than 100,000 tons of tuna yearly, more than anywhere else in Africa. Around Sassandra, fishers set out each day in their long, curved pirogues, or dugout canoes, to fish for catfish, snapper, lobster, and barracuda. Farther inland, river fishers harvest tilapia and catfish.

The city of Daloa in central Côte d'Ivoire is an important center of commerce, where food producers from the north and south meet to exchange grains, vegetables, fruits, meat, milk, eggs, and fish.

Farming for Export

Much of Côte d'Ivoire's farmland is dedicated to cash crops. Although many of the plantations are operated by large agricultural companies, most of the producers are small-scale farmers. Côte d'Ivoire is the world's largest producer of cocoa, producing as much as 1.8 million tons in 2017. The nation exports its cocoa around the world. Sometimes demand is very high and farmers get good prices. Other times, prices fall and farmers frequently look for other ways to earn a living. Many farmers have stopped growing cocoa and turned to growing cashew nuts instead, because cashews can be harvested year-round and profits are higher. Additionally, cashew farmers do less harm to the environment. Unlike cocoa farmers, who clear forests to plant their crops, cashew farmers can plant their orchards in between other trees. Recently, Côte d'Ivoire became one of the leading exporters of cashews, producing more than 700,000 tons each year. Other nuts exported are kola, oil palm, and groundnuts.

Côte d'Ivoire also exports a variety of other foods, including coffee, bananas, and pineapples. Coffee is one of the country's largest exports, with about 100,000 tons sold each year. The country is the twelfth-largest pineapple exporter in the world. Vegetable oils are also exported. Shea butter is produced from the fruit of the karité tree. It is used in soap, in cosmetics, and as a substitute for cocoa butter. Palm oil is also used in soap and cosmetics, as well as in foods such as mayonnaise and bread, and as cooking oil.

Cocoa pods, which contain cocoa beans, often grow directly out of the tree trunk. Each pod weighs about 1 pound (500 grams).

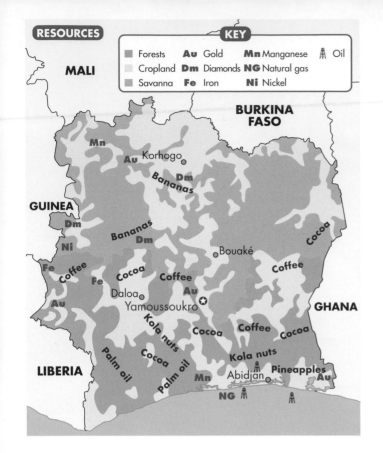

Non-food agricultural exports are rubber, cotton, and tobacco. Cotton has been grown for centuries in Côte d'Ivoire. Farmers export about 400,000 tons of cotton each year. The country is also the world's fifth-largest exporter of natural rubber.

Natural Resources

Côte d'Ivoire is rich in minerals. Mining has gone on since ancient times in West Africa. In Côte d'Ivoire today, there are fewer mines in operation than elsewhere in West Africa because mining companies left during the country's two civil wars. But now, with peace, large mining companies and small-scale miners have returned. They are producing more than 25 tons of gold a year. The gold does not come without a price. Mercury, often used in gold mining, pollutes rivers. Mining engineers are working to reduce pollution.

New technology is also helping small-scale diamond miners. Côte d'Ivoire is a rich source of diamonds, but in 2002, the United Nations banned the country's diamond exports. Called "conflict diamonds" or "blood diamonds," the diamonds mined in Côte d'Ivoire during the civil wars were providing illegal income for rebel forces. The ban was lifted in 2015, and now small-scale diamond mining is supporting the lives of many people in the northern villages. Côte d'Ivoire also mines manganese, iron ore, nickel, cobalt, silica, and bauxite. The country extracts 53,000 barrels of oil a day and 2 billion cubic meters of natural gas a year.

Since the earliest colonial days, Côte d'Ivoire has harvested lumber from its rain forests. Hardwoods such as teak and mahogany were logged and sold, sometimes illegally. Too many trees were cut, and by 1980, Côte d'Ivoire had lost most of its natural timber. Despite the loss, Côte d'Ivoire continues to have a logging industry. Instead of cutting down the rain forests, loggers plant trees such as teak and grasses such as

A geologist studies the rock in a gold-mining region in Côte d'Ivoire. Gold production in the country is growing rapidly. It more than doubled between 2011 and 2016.

bamboo. Once the plants are logged, they are shipped to the ports of Abidjan and San-Pédro. There, workers manufacture plywood, flooring, and sawn wood for furniture making and building construction.

Manufacturing

Côte d'Ivoire is steadily increasing its manufacturing output. The country has a large oil refinery near Abidjan. Some of the oil is processed for use locally while the rest is exported. Côte

Palm oil being poured into a barrel. Côte d'Ivoire is Africa's third-largest producer of the oil, which is used in cooking.

The Past Meets the Future

Many regions around Côte d'Ivoire are renowned for their beautiful fabrics. A specialty of the Senufo people is Korhogo cloth. The cotton is hand spun and handwoven. Weavers weave the cloth in narrow strips, paint them with wax and natural vegetable dyes, and then stitch the strips together. The cloth is prized by many people around the world. Exported Korhogo cloth can be sold for as much as $100 per yard.

Modern technology is helping textile workers create their cloth more efficiently. Mechanical looms and sewing machines make the work faster. Some factories print traditional designs on cloth with ink, but others use traditional wax and dyes. In the world of high fashion, Ivoirian clothing designers are making a mark by designing contemporary clothing inspired by traditional African designs. One of the best known is Loza Maléombho, who creates her designs in a small workshop in a village outside of Abidjan. In 2016, she designed the elaborate African-inspired dress worn by Beyoncé during her Super Bowl halftime performance.

Korhogo cloth is typically colored with earth tones.

d'Ivoire produces machinery and a variety of construction materials, such as concrete, sheet metal, plywood, and ceramics. The cotton textile industry has a long tradition. Thousands of people continue to hand spin cotton into thread, hand dye it, and then handweave it into cloth. However, new factories are using machinery to produce fabrics and clothing.

Food processing is another major industry. Today, the government is urging businesses to process more agricultural products. More jobs are created when workers and growers do more than simply export raw goods. For example, income from cashew production doubles when workers shell, roast, and package the nuts. The same is true for the cocoa industry; more money comes from grinding cocoa beans and making chocolate, rather than just selling cocoa beans. The first cocoa-grinding factory opened in 2015.

What Côte d'Ivoire Grows, Makes, and Mines

Agriculture (2016)

Cocoa beans	1,472,313 metric tons
Cashews	607,300 metric tons
Rubber	310,655 metric tons

Manufacturing (2016, value of exports)

Processed cocoa	$1.8 billion
Refined oil	$563 million
Wood products	$185 million

Mining

Gold (2016)	$503 million in exports
Oil (2016)	53,000 barrels a day
Natural gas (2015)	2 billion cubic meters

Services

The service industry makes up about 68 percent of the economy of Côte d'Ivoire. Service workers are people who do jobs for others, such as teachers, health care workers, taxi drivers, bankers, construction workers, and firefighters. Cities, especially Abidjan, are expanding and creating more service jobs. Tourism has never been a major part of Côte d'Ivoire's economy. But now, a growing number of travelers are attracted to Côte d'Ivoire's palm-lined beaches and deep-sea fishing tours. Tourism opens up new jobs in retail stores, hotels, and restaurants. Additionally, ecotourism is a developing industry, serving visitors to Côte d'Ivoire's rain forests and national parks.

Energy

Côte d'Ivoire is actively increasing its energy supply. The country is producing oil and natural gas at a faster rate, but it still imports most of its fuel. Nearly 15 million people do not

Tourists take part in a music festival in Grand-Bassam.

have electricity. They rely on gas-powered generators. The government is funding many projects to bring electrical power to rural areas and to improve service to cities. Besides numerous diesel-fueled power plants, there are several hydropower dams, including a massive dam on the Sassandra River, which was completed in 2017. Solar power plants are also being built.

Transportation

Côte d'Ivoire has one of the most modern transportation systems in West Africa. There are two major shipping ports that handle nearly 30 million tons of freight each year. There are more than 50,000 miles (80,000 km) of paved roads and an international airport in Abidjan. Construction of new roads, bridges, and railway systems is underway. While cars, taxis, trucks, and buses can cause hours-long traffic jams in Abidjan, rural roads, many of which are not paved, are often traveled by foot, cart, bicycle, and motorbike.

Communication

Côte d'Ivoire has one of the best communications networks in West Africa. More than 25 percent of the population uses the internet. Six cell phone companies operate in Côte d'Ivoire. Together, they have more than twenty-seven million subscribers, more than one for every person in the country. There are few broadcast stations, just two nationwide government-owned television stations, and two radio stations. People prefer listening to the radio. Four national newspapers and several local ones are based in Abidjan.

Money Facts

The West African CFA franc is the currency of Côte d'Ivoire and seven other African countries. CFA is an abbreviation for Communauté Financière Africaine (African Financial Community).

Coins come in denominations of 1, 5, 10, 25, 50, 100, and 500 West African CFA francs. Banknotes are issued in denominations of 500, 1,000, 2,000, 5,000, and 10,000 West African CFA francs. Banknotes and coins feature the image of a brass weight in the form of a catfish called a *taku*. The Asante used the taku as a means of weighing gold dust. It is regarded as a symbol of prosperity.

Banknotes come in a variety of colors. The largest denomination is the 10,000 CFA franc. The banknote is violet and features information technology objects. On the front is the taku

Symbols of education and health are on the front of the 1,000 West African CFA banknote.

symbol and to the right of it is the @ sign, a satellite dish, and a satellite in orbit. On the reverse side are two yellow-billed turacos perched on a branch. In 2018, $1 equaled 572 West African CFA francs.

CHAPTER 7

People and Community

MORE THAN TWENTY-FOUR MILLION PEOPLE LIVE in Côte d'Ivoire. Most Ivoirians have ancestors who immigrated to Côte d'Ivoire from other regions in Africa. Côte d'Ivoire borders the sites of several former empires and kingdoms. As those empires and kingdoms rose and fell, people left and migrated to Côte d'Ivoire. Most came from the Kingdom of Bonoman or the empires of Mali, Songhai, and Kong. Some fled their homelands, while others came seeking land and riches.

Côte d'Ivoire also lay along ancient trade routes. Many traders left the nomadic life to settle in Côte d'Ivoire and establish market centers. When the French colonists arrived, they created borders that split apart traditional ethnic areas. They caused more conflict by forcing people to work on their plantations and by hiring migrant workers from other regions

Opposite: **Many houses in Côte d'Ivoire are round.**

KEY

Ethnic groups
- Akan
- Kru
- Gur
- Mande
- *Koro* Subgroup

MALI

BURKINA FASO

GUINEA

LIBERIA

GHANA

Wojenaka

Senufo
Korhogo ○ *Senufo*

Khisa

Dyula

Senufo

Kulango

Worodougou
Malinke
Koro

Dan

○Bouaké

Guro
Daloa○

Baoulé
✪Yamoussoukro

Anyi

Wé

Bété
Gagu

Anyi

Dida
Abé
Attié

Godiré
Ega
Abidjan●
Anyi

Bakwé

Krumen

and ethnic groups. Several groups in the south and east resisted the French and fought battles well into the twentieth century.

In the nineteenth century, a wave of Lebanese immigrants arrived. Later, in the mid-1970s, Lebanese and Syrian immigrants fled war in their countries and came to Côte d'Ivoire. Many became successful in business, opening shops, hotels, and factories. They are the largest non-African group in the country.

In the years following independence, Côte d'Ivoire's economy was thriving and many immigrants, mostly men from Mali, Guinea, Senegal, and Burkina Faso, came seeking employment. President Félix Houphouët-Boigny welcomed them, calling them "brothers." But after the first civil war, government leaders adopted an anti-immigration policy. Laws were passed denying citizenship to persons who did not have at least one native-born Ivoirian parent. North and south opposed one another again in the second civil war, but after peace was declared, most Ivoirians pledged allegiance to their country.

Ethnic Groups

More than sixty ethnic groups live in Côte d'Ivoire. The nation's four largest ethnic groups are the Akan, Gur, Mande, and Kru.

The Akan make up about 30 percent of the population. They arrived in the tenth century and established gold mining and trading centers. They settled throughout the country, mainly in the central and eastern regions. One Akan subgroup, the Baoulé, is the largest single minority group in the country. They are a matrilineal society, meaning that when a man marries, he joins his wife's family. Children inherit possessions and land through their mother's clan. Baoulé leaders inherit their roles from their mother's side of the family. Many persons from the Baoulé tribe are influential in national government and business.

Lebanese Ivoirians wave the flags of Lebanon and Côte d'Ivoire as they welcome a Lebanese official to Abidjan. Hundreds of thousands of people of Lebanese descent live in Côte d'Ivoire.

Among the Malinke people, the oldest male is the village leader.

The Gur-speaking people live mainly in central Côte d'Ivoire. They include numerous subgroups such as the Gagu and the Senufo. Traditionally, the Gagu people were hunters and gatherers. Today, they do some farming, and many still rely on hunting wild game and collecting fruit and nuts. The Senufo are a large and influential ethnic group. They are expert farmers who work collectively in the fields.

Among the Mande ethnic group are the Malinke, the Soninke, and the Dyula people. Their villages are found across northern Côte d'Ivoire. The Malinke people are a patrilineal society, in which power and possessions pass down through a father's side of the family. The Malinke live in villages made up of grandfathers, fathers, brothers, sons, and their families. The Soninke people traditionally grow crops, raise livestock, and trade in the markets. But many men today leave to do migrant labor elsewhere. Sometimes, the men are gone for years. As a result, many Soninke villages are run by women.

In the Mande language, *dyula* means "trader." The historic market towns of the Dyula people are Kong and Bondoukou. But today, many young Dyula are relocating to Abidjan and other large cities, where there are more business opportunities.

In Côte d'Ivoire, the largest ethnic group within the Kru culture is the Bété. Many coffee and cocoa plantations are owned by Bété farmers. Most Bété communities are small and tend to be independent of other communities. Each village elects a chief based on merit. The chief acts as a spokesperson rather than a ruler. Compared to other ethnic groups, Bété women have traditionally played a more equal role in society. They are included in community decision making, and occasionally a woman is elected chief.

Language

French is the official language of Côte d'Ivoire. It is widely spoken in government, international business, and academic settings. Nearly everyone in Abidjan speaks French, although most speak an informal version of French called Français de Moussa. (Moussa is the name of a cartoon character in an Ivoirian magazine.) Français de Moussa uses borrowed words from native Ivoirian languages, such *as un bra-môgô,*

Ethnicity in Côte d'Ivoire

Akan	32.1%
Mande	22.2%
Gur	15%
Kru	9.8%
Unspecified	0.5%

Non-Ivoirian
(including people from Burkina Faso, Ghana, Guinea, Mali, Nigeria, Benin, Senegal, Liberia, Mauritania, France, Lebanon, and Syria)
21.2%

Some French Phrases

English	French
How are you?	Comment allez-vous?
I am well, thank you.	Je suis bien, merci.
hello	bonjour
good-bye	au revoir, adieu
please	s'il vous plait
yes	oui
no	non

Nouchi

Nouchi is a French slang language used in Côte d'Ivoire, mainly among young people. It originated as street slang, but has slowly moved into wider usage. Nouchi has many sources, including French, Dyula, Baoulé, Bété, Spanish, and English. It is frequently the language used in comedy, popular music, and cell phone texting. Some examples include:

Bingo—term meaning France or another Western country

binguiste or *binguiss*—Ivoirian living or having lived in the West

chap chap—quickly

meaning "dude," and *une go*, meaning "girl," both taken from the Malinke language.

Elsewhere, people speak their ethnic language, along with some French. Each ethnic subgroup has a language or dialect that is related to one of four main language groups, Kwa (the language of the Akan), Mande, Gur, or Kru.

City and Country

More than half the population of Côte d'Ivoire lives in a city or town, and slightly more than one-quarter lives in the largest city, Abidjan. The rest of the population lives in small villages.

Abidjan is one of Africa's largest and most fashionable and modern cities. In the core of the city are high-rise office and apartment buildings, government buildings, hospitals, banks, department stores, theaters, museums, and restaurants. Nearly 90 percent of all the businesses and schools of higher learning in Côte d'Ivoire are located in Abidjan, providing more employment

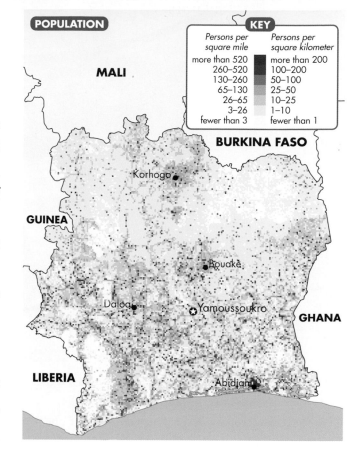

than anywhere else in the country. Other cities along the coast also offer modern conveniences. Many elegant homes and resorts line the lagoons and beaches. The outskirts of Abidjan are growing quickly, but there is inadequate housing and a lack of fresh water and electricity. Many people there are often unemployed.

In rural areas, most homes are constructed with mud, straw, or brick. Roofs are tin or conical-shaped thatch. Some more prosperous villagers, such as the Baoulé, build rectangular concrete homes. Many villages are walled or fenced. The Soninke people build brick rectangular houses with flat roofs and interior courtyards. Their houses line the main street and a mosque is

People demonstrate how to put a mosquito net over a bed. Malaria is the leading cause of death in Côte d'Ivoire.

Beware the Bite

West Africa is home to some of the world's most dangerous diseases, including malaria, polio, cholera, and yellow fever. The government and aid organizations are trying to expand health clinics into more rural communities. They want to vaccinate children and provide villagers with medicines and mosquito nets. Mosquitoes can carry the germs for malaria, and simply sleeping with a mosquito net greatly reduces the chance of getting the disease.

Population of Major Cities (2014)	
Abidjan	4,395,243
Bouaké	536,719
Daloa	245,360
Korhogo	243,048
Yamoussoukro	
	212,670

usually in the village square. A Mande group called the Dan paints murals on their mud homes using red and white clay.

Most villages do not have electricity, running water, or sanitation systems. Villagers who do not live near towns have poor access to health care. Children often travel long distances to get to school. Many quit school early, especially girls, to work to help their families. Tens of thousands of children under the age of fifteen have jobs on plantations or in the mines. Young girls are forced to become *petites bonnes* (little maids) and are sent to work in wealthier homes as domestic servants.

Education

Primary school education in Côte d'Ivoire is free. Parents, however, must pay for books, uniforms, and supplies. Since the government stopped charging school fees, there has been a 60 percent increase in enrollment. Nearly 90 percent of children begin attending school at age six. Three-quarters of students complete primary school, which lasts six years. Secondary school (high school) lasts another four years. Students who plan to go to college often pay for expensive private schools.

Less than 10 percent of Ivoirian students attend a college or university. Most colleges and universities in Côte d'Ivoire are located in Abidjan, but there is one each in Man, Bouaké, Yamoussoukro, Daloa, and Korhogo.

In Côte d'Ivoire, all classes are taught in French.

CHAPTER 8

Faith and Ritual

M ANY IVOIRIANS ARE SPIRITUAL PEOPLE, BUT THE nation has no official religion. The constitution of 2016 grants freedom of religion and states that religious tolerance is vital to a healthy nation.

Two major religions are practiced in Côte d'Ivoire—Islam and Christianity. Most Ivoirians also have a deep connection to the indigenous faith of their ancestors. Among some ethnic groups, indigenous, or native, religions are commonly practiced. Ancient rituals and ceremonies are held in both town and village.

Opposite: **Women enter a mosque made from baked mud in Kong, in northern Côte d'Ivoire.**

Indigenous Faith

The indigenous religions of Côte d'Ivoire share many beliefs. Most people believe in a supreme being, or creator. The Senufo people believe in two supreme beings, Maleeo,

Sacred River

or "Ancient Mother," and Kolotyolo, or "Creator God." Alouroua is the name of the creator god of the Baoulé faith. Asie is the Baoulé god of the Earth, who controls humans and animals. Nature—lakes, rivers, trees, mountains, the sky, and animals—are deeply respected, and people believe spirits live within them. Most villages have a sacred forest or secret place where gods and spirits may live.

Most indigenous faiths in Côte d'Ivoire believe humans have an eternal soul. People revere their families and ancestors. Many rituals include offerings and prayers to them. Ivoirians believe respect to ancestors will keep believers safe and bring them closer to god.

Each group practicing an indigenous religion relies on a spiritual leader to preside over rituals and offer guidance and protection from evil. Holy men and women are believed to have supernatural powers and can communicate with the spirit world. Many rituals are elaborate dances accompanied by rousing music and drumming. Holy men and women fall into trances that take them on spiritual journeys. When they return, it is believed they may be able to tell the future, heal the sick, or give advice to solve a problem. In some Akan religions, healing women called Komians perform a ritual dance called the Ahouwe. In their dance, they become possessed by spirits who teach them how to prepare natural medicines to cure the sick.

Religious ceremonial dances are performed by holy men or women. They wear elaborate and colorful costumes, body paint, jewelry, and most importantly, carved wooden masks. The masks are worn to disguise the human face while—it is believed—the wearer is being transported into the spirit world. Masks take many forms. Some are animal masks, which are worn to seek strength and blessings from animal spirits.

Holy women dance at a ceremony in eastern Côte d'Ivoire.

Holy Ground

A village near Abidjan, called Blockauss, is believed by many to be sacred land ruled by the spirit of a beloved ancestral king. During the civil wars, when many parts of Abidjan and nearby communities were being destroyed by fighting, Blockauss was left untouched. The king's spirit was considered so powerful to Ivoirians that the soldiers—whether Catholic, Protestant, Muslim, or indigenous—refused to fight there.

Some are masks that ask ancestor spirits for peace and good fortune, such as a bountiful crop or the birth of many healthy goats. Some masks are meant to terrify and ward off enemies and evil spirits.

Individuals sometimes seek personal guidance from their spiritual leaders. People who have suffered misfortune or who want children or a good job bring offerings and ask for help. Healers often prepare a charm, or amulet, to wear as jewelry or to hang over a doorway. Amulets are made of leather, wood, clay, shell, or stone. They can be carved or painted.

Islam

The religion of Islam was brought to West Africa by Arab traders from the Middle East. The religion first gained acceptance in West Africa during the eleventh century. Malians migrated to northern Côte d'Ivoire and founded the city of Odienné. They introduced Islam to the Senufo people when they established a trading center in Kong, a large Senufo village. Dyula traders also converted to Islam. When they settled in northeastern Côte d'Ivoire, their religion spread among other traders. The Dyula traders founded the city of Bondoukou, which blossomed into an important center for Islamic study.

According to Islamic belief, God, or Allah, delivered his word to the Prophet Muhammad. The messages God sent to Muhammad are said to have been recorded in the holy book, the Qur'an. Muslims, people who follow Islam, practice a set of duties called the Five Pillars of Islam.

More than 40 percent of Ivoirians are Muslim. Traditionally, they lived in northern Côte d'Ivoire, but today, Muslims can be found throughout the country. Large ethnic groups who

Masks are central to the rituals of the Yacouba people of western Côte d'Ivoire. They represent the spirit of ancestors.

St. Paul's Cathedral, a striking Roman Catholic church in Abidjan, was completed in 1985.

Holy Days

Religious holidays in Côte d'Ivoire include both Muslim and Christian holy days. Christian holy days follow the Gregorian calendar, which is used throughout most of the world. Muslim holy days use the Islamic calendar, which is based on the phases of the moon. The Islamic calendar has twelve months, but it is eleven days shorter than the Gregorian calendar. Muslim holy days fall on the same day every year, according to the Islamic calendar, but shift eleven days earlier each year in the Gregorian calendar. Holy days in Côte d'Ivoire include:

March or April	Easter Sunday
39 days after Easter	Day of Ascension
50 days after Easter	Whit Monday
August 15	Assumption Day
November 1	All Saints' Day
December 25	Christmas
12th day of the 3rd Islamic month	Prophet Muhammad's birthday
1st day of the 9th Islamic month	Ramadan begins
27th day of the 9th Islamic month	Laylat al-Qadr (Night of Power)
Last day of the 9th Islamic month	Eid al-Fitr (End of Ramadan)
10th day of the 12th Islamic month	Eid al-Adha (Feast of the Sacrifice)

typically follow Islam include the Dyula, the Malinke, and several subgroups of the Senufo people. Lebanese and Syrian residents are also mostly Muslim.

While imams are the most powerful Islamic leaders, Ivoirian Muslims often look to Islamic clerics called *marabouts* for religious guidance. Marabouts have qualities that are both Muslim and West African and are common in Côte d'Ivoire. Marabouts, who can be men or women, are believed to have mystical powers. They make amulets inscribed with passages

Muslims remove their shoes when they pray.

The Five Pillars of Islam

The most basic duties of Muslims are called the Five Pillars of Islam. They are:

To declare one's faith that there is no god but God, and that Muhammad is his messenger.

To pray five times a day.

To give to charity.

To fast from sunrise to sunset for the holy month of Ramadan (the ninth month of the Islamic calendar).

To make a pilgrimage, if one is able, to the holy city of Mecca, Saudi Arabia, the birthplace of Muhammad.

from the Qur'an that are thought to provide good luck or protect wearers from harm. Sometimes marabouts perform a ritual in which they write words from the Qur'an on a slab of wood. Then they wash the wood in water. The person seeking help from the marabout drinks or bathes in the water to absorb the word of god.

Christianity

Christianity is the belief that Jesus Christ is the son of god. The earliest Christian believers were Roman Catholics. The pope in Rome, Italy, is their religious leader.

French Catholics brought Christianity to Côte d'Ivoire in the seventeenth century. Five priests arrived in Assinie in 1637 hoping to establish a Catholic mission. They left quickly when one of the priests died from malaria. Fifty years later, a group of French people converted two children of an African king. They became the first Catholics of Côte d'Ivoire. Not until the 1800s did Catholic missionaries arrive in any great

A priest talks to a small child at a Catholic mission in eastern Côte d'Ivoire.

number. The first African Roman Catholic mission in Côte d'Ivoire was established in 1895 in Grand-Bassam. From then on, missionaries spread across the southeast and eventually throughout the country. They established missions, schools, and health clinics. Today, most Ivoirian Catholics live in urban centers in the south and southeast.

Throughout history, many people did not accept the Catholic view of Christianity. They became known as Protestants because they protested Catholic practices. In 1924, Methodist Protestants arrived in Côte d'Ivoire. Other Protestant missionaries followed, including Seventh-Day Adventists, Southern Baptists, and Mormons.

Worshippers at an Evangelical church in Abidjan. The number of Protestants in Côte d'Ivoire has been growing in recent years.

At Harris churches, members usually wear white.

Harrism

The first non-Catholic Christian missionary arrived in Côte d'Ivoire in 1913. He was a Liberian named William Wadé Harris. Calling himself a prophet, Harris preached against sins such as adultery and theft. He believed people should avoid accumulating wealth and should abandon their belief in spirit gods, the power of charms, and indigenous rituals. He lived as he preached and was popular among Ivoirians.

Being African, Harris was aware that some Ivoirian societies were matrilineal and not patrilineal. Earlier missionaries preached only to men, believing that was all they needed to do to convert a village. But Harris knew the strength of a woman's influence in many African societies and was the first Christian missionary to preach to women as well. His religion came to be known as Harrism. There are thousands of followers of Harrism to this day.

Places of Worship

Places of worship dot the countryside in Côte d'Ivoire. Villagers of indigenous faiths build altars, shrines, and temples to honor their ancestors and pay tribute to God and the spirit world. The structures are adorned with carvings,

The Baoulé people are known for making elegant figures for rituals.

textiles, sculptures, paintings, amulets, and offerings of valuable personal items, such as knives, jewelry, or pottery. In some Baoulé villages, people believe they lived in a mystical world before birth. In that world, people are joined with a spiritual husband or wife. Statues made of wood, brass, or gold represent the spiritual spouses on Earth and are placed in special shrines.

The largest Catholic church in Africa, and some say in the world, is in Yamoussoukro. Commissioned by President Félix Houphouët-Boigny in 1985, it was modeled after a large church in Rome, Italy. The church, named Notre-Dame de la Paix (Our Lady of Peace), is so prized by Ivoirians that during the civil wars, people sought refuge inside, knowing the church would not be attacked. Thousands of Catholic churches exist in Côte d'Ivoire, ranging from tiny buildings in small villages to large cathedrals in cities such as Bouaké, Daloa, Korhogo, Abidjan, and Odienné. The Cathedral of Saint Paul in Abidjan is a strikingly modern building. It has curved concrete walls and a massive concrete cross suspended by cables over the entrance.

Methodists, Mennonites, Evangelicals, and other Protestant faiths have also established thousands of churches around the country. Like Catholics, Protestant missionaries serve their believers in ways besides providing spiritual guidance; the churches act as community centers. Many Christian missions have established schools and health clinics.

Islam was the first world religion to enter Côte d'Ivoire, and many of the Islamic houses of worship, called mosques, are ancient. A large mosque in Kong is built of mud. It has tall conical pillars with protruding wooden poles. When it rains, mud washes away from the walls and laborers climb on the poles to replace the mud. There are numerous mosques across the north that are made of mud, straw, and dried plants. The Tengrela Mosque was built in 1655. Like the Kong Mosque, the mud washes away. The Tengrela Mosque has been repaired every ten years throughout the centuries by members of the same family. Bondoukou is often called the city of one thousand mosques. Although there are not nearly that many, the minaret towers of mosques can be seen rising throughout the city. The Grand Mosque in Bouaké was built in 1891. It has tall minaret towers capped with onion-shaped domes. The oldest mosque in Côte d'Ivoire, the Samatiguila Mosque, is in the northwest. Also made of mud, it is more than one thousand years old.

Côte d'Ivoire has long been praised for its religious tolerance. For the most part, religion has not divided communities. From urban centers to tiny villages, it is a common sight to see Christian churches, mosques, and indigenous temples in the same neighborhoods. Although many people practice Christianity and Islam, Ivoirians keep close ties to indigenous beliefs and practices.

Religion in Côte d'Ivoire (2014)	
Muslim	42.9%
Catholic	17.2%
Evangelical	11.8%
Methodist	1.7%
Other Christian	3.2%
Indigenous	3.6%
Other religion	0.5%
None	19.1%

CHAPTER 9

Color and Song

S INCE THE EARLIEST TIMES, CÔTE D'IVOIRE HAS BEEN home to dynamic and creative people. Art, music, dance, craft, and storytelling are central to the cultures of the many different ethnic groups that exist there. For thousands of years, people have enriched their lives through religious celebration and ritual. Many of the art forms were originally inspired by religion, but they have also been used to enhance everyday life.

Opposite: **Dancers perform at an arts festival in Abidjan.**

Music

Music is an important part of rituals and celebrations. Many instruments are made from leather, shells, bone, metal, ivory, and clay. Koras (string instruments), harps, flutes, bells, rattles, and trumpets are made from cattle horns, ivory tusks, or wood. Ivoirians play many types of drums, including the

goblet-shaped *djembe*, which produces loud and various sounds, the modern *kpanlogo* drum, and the hourglass-shaped "talking drum," which can make sounds similar to human speech. Traditionally, the talking drum was used in storytelling and to communicate between villages. Most drummers are men, although some Senufo women play a large, intricately carved wooden drum. Women play many other percussion instruments such as the *shekere* (a hollowed gourd covered in netting and beads), a bell called a *karignan*, and the *kese kese* (a woven basket rattle). Groups of singers often accompany musicians.

Many contemporary Ivoirian musicians draw on their long musical heritage. *Wassoulou* is a style of music that blends instruments such as the harp, the djembe, and the *soku*, a traditional fiddle. It is performed by women and it is believed to have influenced American blues music. Wassoulou thrives to this day with performers such as Fatoumata Diawara, whose songs often touch on issues such as women's rights. *Zouglou* music, which bands such as Magic System have made popular in Abidjan, is similar to rap. Its songs are about problems in society. Hip-hop is also popular. Boobah Siddik listened to his mother's traditional Senufo music and developed his own style of hip-hop. His albums have been released internationally. Manu Katché is an internationally successful drummer who performs rock and jazz inspired by his Ivoirian roots.

Reggae music is also popular in Côte d'Ivoire. The first internationally known Ivoirian reggae musician was Alpha Blondy, whose songs encouraged African unity and peace. Tiken Jah Fakoly is a reggae musician from a family of Dyula musicians and storytellers. His political lyrics made him one of Africa's best-selling musicians. Kajeem, a reggae musician from Abidjan, hosts a nationwide radio show and teaches songwriting to young people.

Dance

Like music, dance is a part of most Ivoirian celebrations and religious rituals. Rural groups dance the way their ancestors danced, and modern dancers are influenced by traditional styles. *Kpanlogo* is an athletic style of dance, performed by young people. Musicians play kpanlogo drums along with a variety of other drums as dancers perform powerful acrobatic leaps and spins. Some dances are danced only by women, such as the Malinke Koutouba dance performed before Ramadan

Duel Dancing

Zaouli is a day-long duel between dancers. One dancer wears a wooden mask in the likeness of a half antelope-half leopard creature. The other dancer is his human opponent. As the energy heightens, both dancers and onlookers fall into a frenzy of fear and excitement. At the end of the day, the audience chooses the winner, but only the chief has the strength to speak the winner's name.

A Zaouli dancer in Bouaké

and the Senufo N'Goron dance performed by women wearing feathers and imitating the flight of birds.

Costumes are worn for traditional dance. Dancers wear beads, feathers, ankle bracelets, colorful scarves, and heavy necklaces made of bead, bone, metal, and shells. Some paint their bodies, dance on stilts, or wear masks.

Masks and Sculpture

Traditional Ivoirian crafts are made with an array of rich colors, bold designs, and a variety of materials. Ethnic groups and families specialize in particular art forms. Skills are passed down from generation to generation.

Baoulé, Dan, and Senufo wood-carvers are known for their ceremonial masks. Some are fine and delicate, while others are exaggerated and menacing. The masks represent spirits, ancestors, living humans, and animals. The Bété and Dan people carve grotesque masks with distorted features, horned foreheads, wild eyes, and sharp fangs meant to repel evil. Guro mask makers carve women's faces with bulging foreheads and elaborate hairstyles. Senufo carvers create large geometric-shaped masks of humans and animals.

Many groups carve sculptures using woods such as ebony and acacia. Baoulé sculptors are known for carving monkeys with large jaws and sharp teeth, which are used in rituals. Attié carvers craft intricate wooden "stools of power" for their chiefs.

Camara Demba is a well-known Ivoirian sculptor who blends traditional sculptures of birds and crocodiles with colorful science fiction and Manga comic themes. His work is displayed in galleries throughout Africa, Europe, and the United States.

Senufo sculptors make masks that combine human and animal features. Called Kpelie masks, they are used in many rituals, including funerals.

Textiles, Metalwork, and Pottery

Côte d'Ivoire and other West African countries are widely known for their specialty cloth, Korhogo. The cloth is spun from locally grown cotton and colored using natural dyes. Senufo weavers make the cloth in strips, which are stitched together and dyed using fermented plants. Colors are generally black, brown, and red. Artists stencil symbolic images, such as a Guinea fowl for inner beauty, a goat for male strength, fish for vitality, a snake for the natural world, and birds for freedom. Akan artists make *kente* cloth, known throughout the world as a symbol of African royalty and dignity. The cloth is made from cotton and silk and woven into brightly colored, intricate geometric patterns.

Akan artisans and Koni villagers in northern Côte d'Ivoire are known for their metalwork in gold, silver, bronze, and brass. They make jewelry, masks, sculptures, and ceremonial vessels using a variety of techniques. Akan metalworkers are historically known for small gold and bronze sculptures used to weigh gold dust.

In many societies, only women are potters. Anyi women create elaborate clay pots called *mma*. They are used in funerals and then placed on graves or as shrines in special places in the forest. Bamana potters use netting, corncobs, string, and seedpods to make basketlike designs in the clay. Dyula female potters form vessels as large as 5 feet (1.5 m) tall to store water and grain.

Painting

Ivoirian paintings, sculpture, and photography are on display in galleries in Abidjan and in cities worldwide. Ouattara Watts

Werewere Liking (left) sings at a concert at the arts center she founded.

Village Ki-Yi M'Bock Arts Center

Village Ki-Yi M'Bock, an arts center and theater in Abidjan, was founded by Werewere Liking, a sculptor, playwright, dancer, and theater director. *Ki-yi m'bock* means "ultimate universal knowledge" in Liking's native language, Bassa. Liking has said that she comes from a culture where people believe an artist is not unlike a priest. An artist can lead people to a sense of harmony, beauty, and spirituality. At the center, young artists come from around the country to work together and create their art. Says Liking, the Ki-Yi M'Bock Village is a "movement for the rebirth of African arts, for the birth of a contemporary African culture and for a coming together, and recognition, of the cultures of the black world."

may be the most famous Ivoirian painter. He paints traditional African symbols and adds recycled objects as well as images from other cultures. Another artist, Abdoulaye Diarrassouba, also called Aboudia, makes bright and bold art that resembles

The Trickster God

Some of the world's most popular folktales came to Côte d'Ivoire with the Akan people. Akan griots told tales they called "words of the sky god." The main character was Kwaku Ananse, a trickster spirit that often took the form of a spider. The small spider uses his cunning and wisdom to trick larger creatures. Griots and elders tell Kwaku Ananse stories to children to teach them about moral behavior and the ways of the world. Sometimes griots act out the stories or accompany their storytelling with drumming, singing, and dancing. Enslaved West Africans brought Ananse stories with them to the Americas.

Ananse the spider sits at the center of this talking stick, which was carried by an official Akan storyteller.

street graffiti. Much of his art is political. During the second civil war, he lived and painted inside an underground bomb shelter. He says he wants his paintings to reflect the lives of Abidjan "street kids."

Literature

The rich literary tradition of Côte d'Ivoire is rooted in storytelling. Some Ivoirian cultures honor the village griot, or

Literary Lion

One of Côte d'Ivoire's most beloved authors, Bernard Binlin Dadié, was born in Assinie in 1916. His first works were a collection of poems, retellings of African legends, and a novel called *Climbié* about society in colonial Côte d'Ivoire. He became well known for his travelers' tales as he satirized society in Paris, New York, and Rome. His humorous account of travels in France, *An African in Paris*, is still in print. He founded Côte d'Ivoire's National Drama Studio and became the country's minister of culture in 1961.

Côte d'Ivoire's national award for literature is named after Bernard Binlin Dadié.

storyteller. The skill of a griot is passed from parent to child, and children are taught the craft from a young age. It is the responsibility of the griot to pass along the history of the village, the tales of their ancestors, and the group's time-honored legends.

Today, Côte d'Ivoire is home to many authors, poets, and playwrights. Véronique Tadjo, who grew up in Abidjan, has published many plays, novels, and children's books. Her children's book *Mamy Wata and the Monster* was chosen as one of

one hundred best African books of the twentieth century. Josué Yoroba Guébo is an award-winning poet, essayist, playwright, and novelist. He won his first award for poetry at age thirteen, and in 2017 won the Bernard Dadié national grand prize for literature.

Sports

After long days at work or at school, Ivoirians like to unwind by playing sports. Taking a refreshing swim in a waterfall, river, or the sea is a favorite leisure activity. Playing ball games such as basketball, volleyball, and soccer is another. Soccer in particular is much loved. Children play it in the street, in empty fields, and in city parks. Nationwide, there are soccer leagues for children and adults.

Basketball is growing more popular among young people in Côte d'Ivoire.

Didier Drogba (right) is the all-time leading scorer for Côte d'Ivoire's national soccer team.

The Pride of Côte d'Ivoire

The pride of all Ivoirians is the national soccer team, nicknamed the Elephants. The team is one of Africa's best. The Elephants have won the African soccer championship several times.

Some of the Elephants' star players are known around the world. These include Yaya Touré, Salomon Kalou, and former record-setting superstar Didier Drogba. Drogba's popularity goes beyond sports. After three years of civil war, the Elephants won a huge game against Madagascar. In the locker room, in front of reporters and television cameras, Drogba led the entire team as it dropped to its knees and begged for peace. The impact of Drogba's speech moved the country into peace talks that resulted in ending the war.

CHAPTER 10

Family and Home

L IFESTYLES IN CITIES CAN SEEM VERY DIFFERENT FROM those in villages, but beneath the surface, Ivoirians look at life in similar ways. They share a common love and respect for families and communities. They want peace and harmony and work together to achieve it. People tend to be artistic, energetic, and hardworking.

Opposite: **Women carry goods for sale along the beach in Grand-Bassam.**

Village Life

In rural areas, most people are farmers. Most villages do not have electricity or running water, so women fetch water from communal wells each day. To transport water, food, and other items, women carry baskets and pots balanced on their heads. Some villagers have other jobs, such as making pottery, weaving, woodcarving, blacksmithing, and leatherworking. Other part-time businesses include trading, beekeeping, or raising livestock.

Family and Home 119

In villages, people work together as a community. The land is often owned and worked in common. In Senufo villages, farmers play a game to see how fast a man can hoe a field. It is a great honor to win and be declared a *sambali,* or master farmer. Many village women run a *tontine,* or lending circle. Each month, every woman puts money into a pot, and at the end of the month a different person wins the money. The winner uses the money to buy something for her family such as a cooking pot, a pair of shoes, or school supplies.

Modern houses line the lagoon in Abidjan.

During a game of awalé, onlookers often give players advice.

Let's Play

Awalé is the Akan version of the common African board game mancala. Parents enjoy teaching the game to children to introduce them to arithmetic. Only two people play at a time, but the game always attracts attention and players often ask onlookers for advice.

To play, you need an awalé board. This is a board with six pits on each side and one long pit, called a store, on each end. You can draw your awalé board on cardboard or use an egg carton. You will also need forty-eight playing pieces. These are often seedpods but can be stones or coins.

To begin, two players place four seeds in each pit on their side of the board. The player who goes first picks up all the seeds from one of the pits on his or her side. The player then distributes the pieces, one in each pit, moving counterclockwise. If your last seed lands in your store, you go again. The other player then takes his or her turn. On each turn, if a player drops his or her last seed in the opponent's pit and that pit has two or three seeds, the player takes those seeds and puts them in the store. The game continues until one player has collected twenty-five seeds.

City Life

More than 20 percent of the population lives in Abidjan. People enjoy visiting museums, theaters, parks, and the zoo. Near the city center, many families live in comfortable houses with modern conveniences. On the city outskirts, families

Pottery is among the many kinds of goods sold at markets in Côte d'Ivoire.

tend to be poorer. In these communities, people share kitchens and bathrooms. Children there must often help their families earn a living. After school, they help in shops, food stands, market stalls, or by doing odd jobs. Families in cities tend to have fewer children than rural families.

Clothing

In both rural villages and big cities, people wear vibrant-colored clothing. The most popular item for women is a pagne, which is a large wraparound skirt. Women also wear headscarves, as do some men. Some pagnes are made with wax and dyes and some, called "fancy fabric," are printed. Designs include stars, swirls, flowers, checks, and paisleys. Prints include objects from pop culture, such as lipsticks and cell phones, as well as religious images, political figures, and film stars. Traditional men's garments include a neck scarf, skullcap, and a printed robe called a *boubou*. In cities, people are more likely to dress in Western-style clothes, but many include a colorful flair. Men and boys wear shirts, shorts, and loose pants. Girls wear colorful dresses or pagnes.

Going to Market

Markets are an important part of life in Côte d'Ivoire, regardless of whether a person lives in a city or village. In lively markets, people sell a wide array of clothing, household items, and crafts. Alongside cafés and French bakeries are shops selling fruits and vegetables, meat, poultry, eggs, and dairy products. Markets are a feast for the senses, with the colorful clothing, the music playing, and the delicious aromas coming from *maquis*. Maquis are small open-air restaurants or food stands that sell a tantalizing mixture of Ivoirian foods inspired by French cuisine.

Food

Vegetables, grains, fish, and chicken are all common in Ivoirian meals. *Attiéké* is a mainstay at many meals. It is made by grating up a root vegetable called cassava. Cooks often serve dishes such as spinach stew, grilled chicken, groundnut soup, and fresh fish stew. *Kedjenou* is a flavorful stew made with eggplant, okra, tomatoes, and peanuts. Fried onions, chilis, and ginger spice up many dishes.

In villages, extended families often gather to eat together. Many foods are eaten by hand. People roll attiéké or rice into a thick ball and dip it into bits of meat, vegetables, and sauce. Elders begin eating first, and children are expected to show good table manners. Many meals end with a dessert of fresh fruit, such as pineapple or watermelon.

Festivals and Holidays

Throughout the year, Ivoirians celebrate many different holidays. Both Christian and Muslim holidays are celebrated as public holidays. The Christian holidays include Easter, All Saints' Day, and Christmas. For Christmas, family and friends

A woman strains cassava while making attiéké. Large batches of the attiéké batter are left to dry before being cooked.

Getting Married

Marriage customs differ among the many ethnic groups of Côte d'Ivoire. But these traditions are changing. Many young people have left home to work in towns and cities and no longer follow traditions in the same way as older generations.

One tradition that is still practiced in many communities is the "knocking ceremony." When a couple decides to marry, the groom will speak with his parents and they will visit the bride's family, traditionally bearing gifts of palm wine and money. Today, however, the gifts might include an engagement ring. The bride's parents ask for time to consider the marriage. They research the groom's past before agreeing to the union.

In preparation for the wedding, the bride's family will present a list of all items needed for the ceremony, such as clothing and shoes and jewelry for the bride and her family. Traditionally the father of the groom pays, but in recent times, the groom usually pays for the wedding. In many rural traditions, the groom's father will work for the bride's family or give them money, food, or livestock. Even in cities, it is often still a tradition for the bride to receive a ceremonial basket of clothing.

At the wedding, people dress in either traditional clothing or modern fashions with African patterns and designs. Some brides in urban areas wear white Western-style dresses, but most opt to include traditional wedding bead jewelry, scarves, and hats. Many couples dress in traditional pagnes.

After the wedding ceremony, the bride is often "presented" to the world as a married woman. Her female family members bring her onstage at the reception or into the courtyard where the wedding celebration is being held, and everyone cheers for her. Non-Muslim couples might perform the libation ceremony, in which they pray together and pour wine on the ground in the four directions to honor their ancestors. Then the celebration begins, with music, dancing, and feasting, sometimes for days.

Some brides in Côte d'Ivoire cover their hands with henna tattoos for their wedding day.

gather to enjoy festive foods, music, and dancing. People do not exchange presents until New Year's Day.

The major Muslim holidays include Eid al-Fitr, Eid al-Adha, and the Prophet Muhammad's birthday. Eid al-Fitr is a joyous celebration that marks the end of the fasting during Ramadan. Eid al-Adha is also known as the Feast of the Sacrifice. On this day, families slaughter a goat or sheep and divide it into thirds. One-third is for the family, one-third is for friends, and the last third is given to charity. People then gather and enjoy a feast. In Abidjan, it is custom to visit the zoo on this holiday.

Ivoirians celebrate Independence Day on August 7 with parades, speeches, music, and dance. Other public holidays are National Peace Day and Labor Day.

Public Holidays

January 1	New Year
March or April	Easter Sunday
May 1	Labor Day
May or June	Day of Ascension
May or June	Whit Monday
August 7	Independence Day
August 15	Assumption of Mary
November 1	All Saints' Day
November 15	National Peace Day
December 25	Christmas Day
12th day of the 3rd Islamic month	Prophet Muhammad's birthday
1st day of the 9th Islamic month	Ramadan begins
27th day of the 9th Islamic month	Laylat al-Qadr (Night of Power)
Last day of the 9th Islamic month	Eid al-Fitr
10th day of the 12th Islamic month	Eid al-Adha (Feast of the Sacrifice)

Ivoirians also hold many ethnic festivals. The biggest is the Festival of Masks held in November near the city of Man. The festival attracts villagers from all around the country who wear their best masks and compete in dancing competitions. Bouaké hosts a twenty-four-hour festival called Goli a few times a year, which also celebrates masks. One type of mask is called the *kpan*. The festival begins with women singing and dancing and calling for the masks to come. When the kpan mask dancers arrive, the women drape them with scarves and dance and sing around them. The Baoulé people also host a carnival that attracts dancers and musicians from all over Africa. At the carnival, Ivoirians enjoy the performances and admire the art. They also feast together at communal tables, celebrating life and friendship.

Timeline

Côte d'Ivoire History

4500–2000 BCE
Early peoples in the Côte d'Ivoire region produce artifacts.

700s CE
North African Berber nomads begin trading in the region.

1100s
Dyula people migrate into Côte d'Ivoire; Senufo people establish Korhogo.

1200s
The Mali Empire spreads into Côte d'Ivoire.

Late 1400s
European traders begin buying or enslaving West Africans and taking them to the Americas.

1482
Portuguese traders arrive in the region.

1637
The French establish a mission at Assinie.

1700s
Queen Abla Pokou founds the Baoulé kingdom.

1878
Samory Touré founds the Wassoulou Empire.

1885
European powers hold the Berlin Conference a which they discuss how to divide up Africa.

1893
Côte d'Ivoire becomes a French colony.

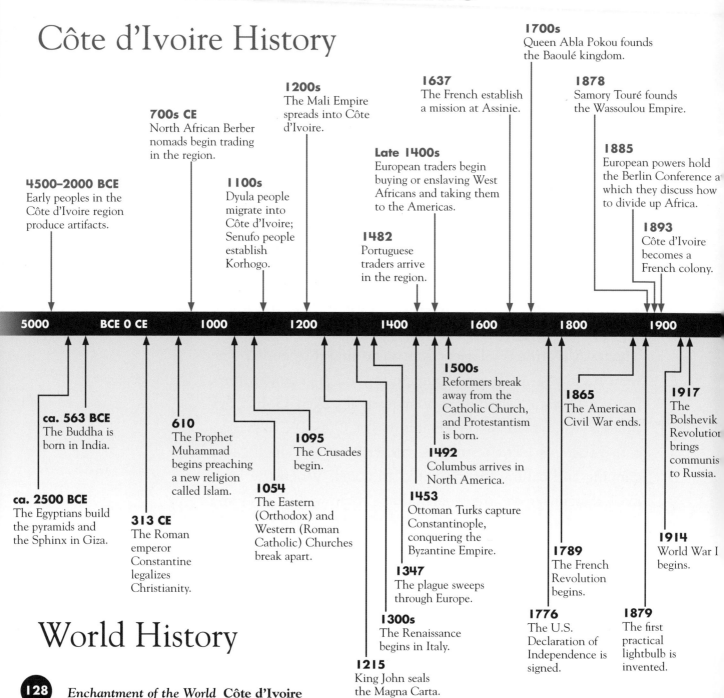

5000   BCE 0 CE   1000   1200   1400   1600   1800   1900

ca. 2500 BCE
The Egyptians build the pyramids and the Sphinx in Giza.

ca. 563 BCE
The Buddha is born in India.

313 CE
The Roman emperor Constantine legalizes Christianity.

610
The Prophet Muhammad begins preaching a new religion called Islam.

1054
The Eastern (Orthodox) and Western (Roman Catholic) Churches break apart.

1095
The Crusades begin.

1215
King John seals the Magna Carta.

1300s
The Renaissance begins in Italy.

1347
The plague sweeps through Europe.

1453
Ottoman Turks capture Constantinople, conquering the Byzantine Empire.

1492
Columbus arrives in North America.

1500s
Reformers break away from the Catholic Church, and Protestantism is born.

1776
The U.S. Declaration of Independence is signed.

1789
The French Revolution begins.

1865
The American Civil War ends.

1879
The first practical lightbulb is invented.

1914
World War I begins.

1917
The Bolshevik Revolution brings communis to Russia.

World History

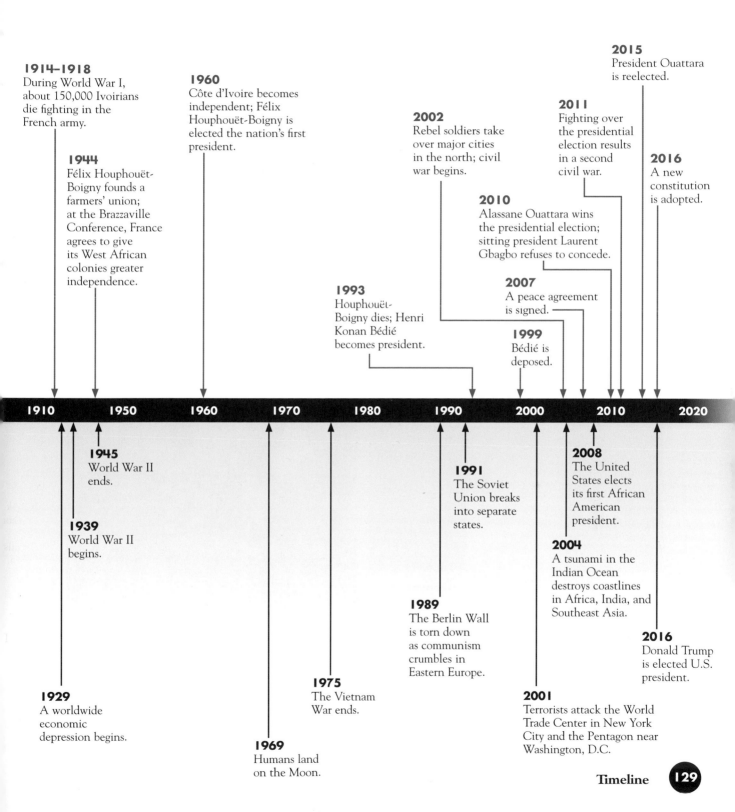

1914–1918
During World War I, about 150,000 Ivoirians die fighting in the French army.

1944
Félix Houphouët-Boigny founds a farmers' union; at the Brazzaville Conference, France agrees to give its West African colonies greater independence.

1960
Côte d'Ivoire becomes independent; Félix Houphouët-Boigny is elected the nation's first president.

2015
President Ouattara is reelected.

2011
Fighting over the presidential election results in a second civil war.

2016
A new constitution is adopted.

2002
Rebel soldiers take over major cities in the north; civil war begins.

2010
Alassane Ouattara wins the presidential election; sitting president Laurent Gbagbo refuses to concede.

1993
Houphouët-Boigny dies; Henri Konan Bédié becomes president.

2007
A peace agreement is signed.

1999
Bédié is deposed.

1910   1950   1960   1970   1980   1990   2000   2010   2020

1945
World War II ends.

1939
World War II begins.

1991
The Soviet Union breaks into separate states.

2008
The United States elects its first African American president.

2004
A tsunami in the Indian Ocean destroys coastlines in Africa, India, and Southeast Asia.

1929
A worldwide economic depression begins.

1989
The Berlin Wall is torn down as communism crumbles in Eastern Europe.

2016
Donald Trump is elected U.S. president.

1975
The Vietnam War ends.

2001
Terrorists attack the World Trade Center in New York City and the Pentagon near Washington, D.C.

1969
Humans land on the Moon.

Timeline   129

Fast Facts

Official name of the country:	Republic of Côte d'Ivoire
Capital:	Yamoussoukro
Official language:	French
Official religion:	None
Independence:	August 7, 1960
National anthem:	"L'Abidjanaise" ("The Song of Abidjan")
Type of government:	Presidential republic
Head of state:	President
Head of government:	Prime minister

Left to right: **National flag, local chief**

MALI

BURKINA FASO

GUINEA

Odienné Korhogo Ferkessédougou

Kongo Comoé N.P.

EUROPE ASIA
Area of map
AFRICA

Touba Séguéla Bondoukou

Mt. Nimba Strict
Nature Reserve

Bouaké

CÔTE D'IVOIRE

Man Marahoué N.P. Yamoussoukro

Daloa Bouaflé Abengourou

GHANA

Toumodi Dimbokro

Guiglo

N
W   E
S

Gagnoa Agboville

LIBERIA Soubré Divo

Tai N.P. Tanoé-Ehy
National Forest

Assagny N.P. Abidjan Bingerville

Sassandra Grand-Lahou Grand-Bassam Assinie

ATLANTIC OCEAN

San-Pédro Gulf of Guinea

0   100 MI
0   100 KM

Abidjan

Area of country:	124,502 square miles (322,460 sq km)
Bordering countries:	Liberia and Guinea to the west, Mali and Burkina Faso to the north, and Ghana to the east
Highest elevation:	Mount Nimba, 5,748 feet (1,752 m) above sea level
Lowest elevation:	Sea level along the coast
Average high temperature:	In Yamoussoukro, 85°F (30°C) in February, 78°F (25.5°C) in August
Average low temperature:	In Yamoussoukro, 77°F (25°C) in February, 73°F (23°C) in August
Average annual ocean temperature:	82°F (28°C)
Average annual precipitation:	Yamoussoukro, 44 inches (112 cm)

National population (2014):	24,184,810	
Population of major cities (2014):	Abidjan	4,395,243
	Bouaké	536,719
	Daloa	245,360
	Korhogo	243,048
	Yamoussoukro	212,670

Landmarks:
- ▶ *Basilica of Our Lady of Peace*, Yamoussoukro
- ▶ *Cathedral of Saint Paul*, Abidjan
- ▶ *Samatiguila Mosque*, Samatiguila
- ▶ *Taï National Park*, western border along Cavally River
- ▶ *Zadépleu waterfall*, Man

Economy: Two-thirds of workers in Côte d'Ivoire are engaged in agriculture. Besides farming, raising livestock, and fishing, many farmers work on commercial plantations producing cocoa, coffee, rubber, and palm oil. Côte d'Ivoire is the world's largest exporter of cocoa beans. Gold mining and oil extraction are other important industries.

Currency: Côte d'Ivoire and seven other African nations use the West African CFA franc. CFA is an abbreviation for Communauté Financière Africaine (African Financial Community). In 2018, $1 equaled 572 West African CFA francs.

System of weights and measures: Metric system

Literacy rate: 43%

French words and phrases:

yes	*oui*
no	*non*
How are you?	*Comment allez-vous?*
I am well, thank you.	*Je suis bien, merci.*
hello	*bonjour*
good-bye	*au revoir, adieu*

Prominent Ivoirians:

Bernard Binlin Dadié	(1916–)
Novelist, poet, and playwright	
Abdoulaye Diarrassouba	(1983–)
Painter	
Didier Drogba	(1978–)
Soccer player	
Félix Houphouët-Boigny	(1905–1993)
First president of Côte d'Ivoire	
Loza Maléombho	(1985–)
Clothing designer	
Queen Abla Pokou	(ca. 1730–ca. 1750)
Founder of Baoulé Empire	

Clockwise from top: **Currency, Didier Drogba, schoolchildren**

To Find Out More

Books

▶ *African Masters: Art from the Ivory Coast.* Chicago: University of Chicago Press, 2015.

▶ Conrad, David. *Empires of Medieval West Africa.* New York: Chelsea House, 2009.

▶ Drogba, Didier. *Commitment: My Autobiography.* London: Hodder & Stoughton, 2016.

▶ Hobbs, Annelise. *West Africa.* Broomall, PA: Mason Crest Publishers, 2017.

Music

▶ *African Pearls: Côte d'Ivoire, West African Crossroads.* Paris: Syllart Records, 2010.

▶ Alpha Blondy. *Positive Energy.* New York: VP Records, 2015.

▶ *Côte d'Ivoire: Baule Vocal Music.* Washington, D.C.: Smithsonian Folkways, 2014.

▶ Magic System. *Africainement Votre.* New York: Warner, 2014.

▶ Visit this Scholastic website for more information on Côte d'Ivoire:
www.factsfornow.scholastic.com
Enter the keywords **Ivory Coast**

Location of Côte d'Ivoire

Index

Page numbers in *italics* indicate illustrations.

military, *52*, 53, 59
mining, 43, 50, 52, 74–75, *75*, 78, 90
missionaries, 101–102, 103, 104–105
mma (clay pots), 112
mosques, 89–90, *92*, 105
mosquitoes, 90, *90*
Mount Nimba, 16, 19, 22–23, 31
Mount Nimba Strict Nature Reserve, 22–23
Muhammad (Islamic prophet), 97, 100, 126
music, 49, 67, 94, 107–109, *108*, *113*, 125, 126, 127

N
national anthem, 67
National Assembly, 58, 59, 66, *66*
national bird, 34, *34*
National Chamber of Kings and Traditional Chiefs, 68
National Drama Studio, 115
national flag, 65, *65*
national flower, 32, *32*
national holidays, 124, 127
national language, 7
national parks, 21–22, *23*, 37, 38, 39, 79
natural gas, 75, 79
Nazi Party, 54
newspapers, 81
New Year's Day, 126
Notre-Dame de la Paix (Our Lady of Peace), *69*, 69, 104
Nouchi language, 88

O
Odienné, 43, 44, 96
oil industry, 75, 76, 79
Ouattara, Alassane, 10–11, 60, 61, *61*

P
pagnes (clothing), 13, 122–123, 125
paintings, 112–114

palm oil, 25, 58, 73, 76
Pango, Pierre-Michel, 67
people. *See also* women.
   Abron, 44
   Akan, 43–44, 84–85, 87, 94, 112, 114, *114*
   ancestors, 94, 96, 109, 111, 125
   Anyi, 44, 112
   Asante, 44, 81
   Baoulé, 13, 44, 45, *45*, 89, 94, 104, *104*, 110, 111, 127, 133
   Berber, 41–42, *42*
   Bété, 87, 111
   children, 11–12, 85, 90, 91, *91*, 96, 122, 124
   clothing, 6, 13, *70*, 77, *103*, 110, 122–123, 125
   Dan, 90, 110, 111
   Dyula, 42, 44, 86, 87, 96, 99, 109
   early people, *40*, 41, 83
   education, 7, 10, 11, 53, 64, 89, 90, 91, *91*
   employment, 59, *70*, 90, 122
   foods, 31, 123–124, *124*
   forced labor, 51, 52–53, 54
   Gagu, 41, 86
   Gur, 84, 86, 87
   Guro, 111
   health care, 29, 30, 31, 32, 90, 95
   housing, *11*, *82*, 89–90, *120*, 121–122
   immigrants, 25, 84, 87
   knocking ceremony, 125
   Koni, 112
   Kru, 45, 71, 84, 87
   languages, 7, 42, 49, 52, 53, 86, 87–88, *91*, 113
   Lebanese, 84, 85
   libation ceremony, 125
   Mali Empire, 43, 44
   Malinke, 42, 51, 86, *86*, 99
   Mande, 84, 86–87
   marriage, 125, *125*

population, 25, 69, 89
Portuguese traders, 8, 46–47
poverty, 61
rural areas, 89–90, 119–120
Senufo, 12–13, 40, 43, 72, 77, *77*, 86, 93–94, 96, 99, 108, 109, 110, 111, *111*, 112, 120
slavery, 46, *46*, 47, 48, 51
Songhai, 44
Soninke, 42–43, 86–87, 89–90
Syrian, 84
urban areas, 89, 121–122
vaccinations, 90
voting rights, *62*
Yacouba, 97
pirogue (canoe), *20*
plantations, 49
plant life
   acacia trees, 31
   baobab trees, 31
   bromeliads, 30
   coastline, 27–28
   Daloa, 25
   diversity of, 27
   Eighteen Mountains region, 31
   emergent trees, 30
   erosion and, 28
   grasses, 30
   health care and, 29, 30, 31, 32, 95
   kapok trees, 30
   karité trees, 31, 73
   kola nuts, 30, *30*
   lantana flower, 32, *32*
   liana vines, *14*
   limba trees, 29
   logging industry, *22*, 50, 75–76
   mangrove trees, 18, 19, 27–28
   rain forests, 21, 28, 29–30, 44–45
   rubber trees, 28, *28*
   savanna region, 30–31
   tourism and, 39
   trees, 28, *28*, 29–30, 31, 75–76

tourism, 7, 39, 79, *79*
towns. *See also* cities; villages.
    Assinie, 48, 49, 101, 115
    Bingerville, 18
    Bonoua, *126*
    Grand-Bassam, 18, 19, 49, 79, 102,
      118
    Grand-Lahou, 19, *19, 20*
    Kong, 43, 44, 51, 87, *92*, 96, 105
trade, 8, 42–43, *43–44*, 46, 83
transportation, 9, 25, 50, 80

U
United Nations (UN), 60
United States, 8, 47, 58

V
vaccinations, 90
Vichy government, 54, 56
Village Ki-Yi M'Bock arts center, 113,
    113
villages. *See also* cities; towns.
    Blockauss, 96
    employment in, 119
    foods in, 123–124

religion in, 94, 96, 103–104
storytellers in, 114–115, *114*
water and, 119
voting rights, *62*

W
Wassoulou Empire, 42, 51
wassoulou music, 108–109
Watts, Ouattara, 112–113
weaverbirds, 35
West African CFA franc (currency), 81,
    81
wetlands, 18, 19, 27–28, 32, 94
white-cheeked turaco (national bird),
    34, *34*
wildflowers, 30–31, 32, *32*
wildlife. *See* animal life; insect life;
    marine life; plant life; reptilian life.
women. *See also* people.
    clothing, 13, 122
    dance and, *95*, 109, 110
    Goli festival and, 127
    government and, *62*, 87
    lending circles, 120
    music and, 108, 109

pottery, 13, 112
religion and, 94–95, *95*, 99, 103
water and, 119
World War I, *52*, 53
World War II, 53–54

Y
Yacouba people, 97
Yamoussoukro. *See also* cities.
    Basilica of Our Lady of Peace, 69,
      69, 104
    as capital city, 69
    climate of, 16
    crocodiles in, *36*
    education, 91
    map of, 69
    name origin, 69
    population, 69, 90
Yopougon suburb, 9

Z
Zadépleu waterfall, 20, *21*
Zaouli dance, 110, *110*
zoos, 126

Meet the Author

Ruth Bjorklund grew up in rural New England where she went hiking, rowing, and sailing. She left New England, traveled, and eventually settled in Seattle, Washington, where she attended the University of Washington. There, she earned a bachelor's degree in comparative literature and a master's degree in library and information science.

She has been a children's and young adult librarian and has written many books on a wide range of subjects, including the history, geography, and culture of states and countries, health, endangered animals, and contemporary issues.

Today, Bjorklund lives on Bainbridge Island, a ferry ride away from Seattle. She enjoys kayaking, sailing, camping, and traveling.

Photo Credits